Biblical Thinking for Building Healthy Churches

info@9marks.org | www.9marks.org

Tools like this are provided by the generous investment of donors.
Each gift to 9Marks helps equip church leaders with a biblical vision and practical resources for displaying God's glory to the nations through healthy churches.

Donate at: www.9marks.org/donate.

Or make checks payable to "9Marks" and mail to:
9 Marks
525 A St. NE
Washington, DC 20002

Editorial Director: Jonathan Leeman
Editor: Sam Emadi
Managing Editor: Alex Duke
Layout: Rubner Durais
Cover Design: OpenBox9
Production Manager: Rick Denham & Mary Beth Freeman
9Marks President: Mark Dever
Paperback: 978-1-958168-16-5
eBook: 978-1-958168-17-2

5 Editor's Note

REVIVAL & REVIVALISM THEN

9 Six Marks of Revivalism
by Andrew S. Ballitch

15 What Can We Learn from Charles Spurgeon and the New York Revival of 1858?
by Geoff Chang

25 Finney with a Twist: Elder Jacob Knapp and the Origins of Baptist Revivalism
by Caleb Morell

34 Edwards, Revival, and the Necessary Means of Prayer
by Mark Rogers

41 Revival Comes to Washington
by Caleb Morell

49 Forgotten, Real Revivals of the Second Great Awakening
by Mark Rogers

REVIVAL & REVIVALISM NOW

57 Pentecost: An Earthquake with Ongoing Tremors
by Sinclair Ferguson

59 Don't Walk the Aisle, Carry Your Cross
by Ben Lacey

64 Can You Reverse Engineer Revival?
by Sean DeMars

68 How Strong Trellises Promote Strong Vines
by Paul Alexander

72 Pray for Revival—in the Other Guy's Church
by Andy Johnson

REVIVALISM AND MINISTRY

76 How Movements Can Undermine Churches and Hurt Their Own Cause
by Jonathan Leeman

| 82 | **Why Revivalism Causes Pastors to Burn Out and Job-Hop**
by Phil A. Newton

| 87 | **The Revival We Need and the Unregenerate Church Members We Have**
by Jim Elliff

| 93 | **Revivalism on the Mission Field**
by Scott Logsdon

| 101 | **Revival and Revivalism in Youth Ministry**
by Mike McGarry

| 104 | **The Worship Set: Today's Sawdust Trail**
by Drew Hodge

ELDER MEDITATION: "AN ELDER MUST BE ABOVE REPROACH"

| 109 | **Is Being Above Reproach a Qualification?**
by Jeffrey Jeffson

| 114 | **What Does Being 'Above Reproach' Mean?**
by Paul Alexander

| 116 | **How 'Above Reproach' Lay Elders Saved My Ministry**
by Gary Kirst

| 118 | **Why Is Being Above Reproach Necessary in Hard Times?**
by David Doran

| 120 | **Why Does a Pastor Being 'Above Reproach' Matter?**
by Peter Hess

BOOK REVIEWS

| 123 | **Book Review: *The Heart of the Gospel: A.B. Simpson, the Fourfold Gospel, and Late Nineteenth-Century Evangelical Theology*, by Bernie A. Van De Walle**
Reviewed by Kevin Niebuhr

| 128 | **Book Review: *Revival and Revivalism: The Making and Marring of American Evangelicalism, 1750-1858*, by Iain Murray**
Reviewed by Bobby Jamieson

Editor's Note:

PURSUING REVIVAL WHILE AVOIDING REVIVALISM

By Jonathan Leeman

D ifferent groups of pastors often have their favorite books. Sometimes those books provide the vocabulary for how those groups talk and think. Folks in my circles often use the language of *revival versus revivalism* to describe two different ways of doing ministry. We take it from Iain Murray's 1994 book *Revival and Revivalism: The Making and Marring of American Evangelicalism 1750–1858* (see our summary and review here).

Murray characterizes America's First Great Awakening as characterized by the kind of revivals we find in the Bible (on understanding revivals biblically, see Sinclair Ferguson's article). Murray borrows Solomon Stoddard's definition: "Some special seasons wherein God doth in a remarkable manner revive religion among his people" (xvii). Biblical revivals of this sort depend instrumentally on the ordinary means of grace, but ultimately upon God's decision and action. Churches will do what they always do: proclaim the gospel, confess their sins, and pray for God to save sinners. Yet God decides to act in a remarkable manner—"The wind blows wherever it pleases" (John 3:8). True revivals are always "surprising," to borrow a word from Jonathan Edwards.

Yet in the last forty years of the nineteenth century, says Murray referring to the latter parts of the Second Great Awakening, "a new view of revival came generally to displace the old." He continues:

> Seasons of revival became 're-vival meetings.' Instead of being 'surprising' they might now be even announced in advance, and whereas no one in the previous century had known of ways to secure a revival, a system was not popularized by 'revivalists' which came near to guaranteeing results. (xviii)

This new view Murray calls revival*ism*. And the long and short of it from our perspective is revivals are good; revivalism is bad—bad for producing true conversions and bad for the long-term good of churches.

Though history is a little too complicated to say the First Great Awakening was characterized entirely by revivals, while the Second Great Awakening was characterized entirely by revivalism, as Mark Rogers will argue in his piece, the language of revival and revivalism does provide two poles for how to do ministry.

Revivalism, built on non-Reformed assumptions about depravity and regeneration, treats people as *drowning*. Sinners are "dead" in trespasses and sins, but not so "dead," apparently, they cannot hear the person in the boat saying, "Grab my hand." The person in the boat, meanwhile, should do everything possible—argue, persuade, cajole, even manipulate—to get the person to grab the outreached hand. Use psychological pressure. Use social pressure. Get the cool kids to set an example. Talk about citywide "tipping points." Whatever! Just get people to grab the hand.

Revival, built on a reformed understanding of depravity and regeneration, treats people not as drowning but as *drowned*. To say people are spiritually "dead" means they're spiritually "dead." As in, not breathing. As in, lean over the boat and scream all you want, the person cannot hear you. Only when the Spirit comes and regenerates can a person hear and respond. Word and Spirit must work together, like Ezekiel in the Valley of dry bones. Ezekiel's preaching isn't enough. The *ruach—breath, wind, Spirit—*had to blow (Ezek. 37:8-11).

Where revivalism depends on God's Words *plus* our methods, revival depends on God's Word.

Or to unpack that: where revivalism depends on extraordinary means of human ingenuity, revival depends on the ordinary means of grace prescribed in the Bible, like preaching and praying. Where revivalism relies on the powers of human psychology and sociology, revival relies on Word and Spirit. Where revivalism emphasizes creativity and charisma, revival emphasizes contrition and submission. And, therefore, where revivalism tends to bring glory to our innovations, revival brings glory to God.

Revival's emphases, mind you, don't decry the use of means. Preachers must study, work hard, master languages and grammar, devise sentences and paragraphs, and engage in a whole host of everyday, human activities. It doesn't say all creativity and charisma are bad. God will use such gifts, even as he uses various psychological and social forces. The question, pastor, is what are you actively seeking to *build* on? God's Word or God's Word *plus* your methods?

If the latter, you may have forgotten what makes Christian disciple-making unique relative to every other form of disciple-making—it aims to accomplish something that simply is not within our power to accomplish: giving life to the dead, or causing people to be born again. When we evangelize, says Mark Dever, we're evangelizing the graveyard.

Three lessons result: One, all our disciple-making is dependent on God in a way nothing else is. Two, the best means are only those means he prescribes in his Word. Three, we must never idolize the human actors even when God uses them mightily, as made evident by the complicated legacies of George Whitefield and Jonathan Edwards, who sinfully and tragically affirmed race-based slavery.

Yet these are lessons we quickly forget, which is why so much ministry today, whether on college campuses or in church services, ends up being revivalistic. Pastors plant church members in the audience who will walk forward during an altar call so that others will follow. Writers argue that if 12 percent of New Yorkers come to know Christ, the city will have reached a tipping point and the dam will burst. Professors devote entire chapters to the value of creativity in books on church structure. Preachers employ heart-gripping illustrations or heart-harrowing statistics and then lean into the imperatives for what people must *do*. Worship leaders cycle choruses round and round until the swell of emotion creates a new sense of intimacy with Jesus.

Our goal with this Journal is to help you as pastors, ministry leaders, and missionaries better recognize these two ways of doing ministry, that you might better rely on the Lord to serve the Lord. Revivalism, which depends on our ingenuity and energy, brings short-term gains. It looks fruitful. It appeals to our yearning to *see* the results of our labors. You can watch the numbers explode.

Yet often that fruit is fake. And we don't want you to be fooled, because when pastors are fooled, the people behind the conversion statistics gain false assurance. They walk toward an eternity apart from Christ while calling themselves Christians all the way.

Revival, however, builds for the long-term. It walks by faith. It doesn't expect to see all the fruit of our labors now but trusts that God is doing far more than we expect with every act of ministry, like what old George Bailey (Jimmy Stewart) discovers about his own work by the end of *It's a Wonderful Life*.

This Journal means to provide the lens for distinguishing one kind of ministry from the other. When you're done with it, turn back to our Journal on the Ordinary Means of Grace (July 2021) to learn more about building for Revival.

Six Marks of Revivalism

By Andrew S. Ballitch

Modern evangelicalism emerged out of the series of revivals that took place in America and Britain from the 1730s through the 1830s, revivals which have left an indelible mark on the contemporary movement. The surprising work of God that took place in New England during the ministries of men such as Jonathan Edwards and George Whitefield gave way to unprecedented, exponential growth of the Methodists and Baptists on the American frontier around the turn of the century. At the same time, other denominations and sects expanded along the colonial coast and elsewhere in the fledgling United States. This makes it difficult to neatly separate the First and Second Great Awakenings.

During the First Great Awakening Edwards had struck a careful balance that legitimized emotional expression and outward manifestation during times of revival without using them as the movement's measuring stick. By the 1820s, this careful balance had began to be supplanted by revivalism.

This revivalism was by no means monolithic. Nonetheless, it had many consistent marks. Below I will offer six: reverse engineering, celebrity cults of personality, a reliance on high production quality, emotional manipulation, reductionist views of conversion, and inadequate ecclesiology. This list is certainly not exhaustive; nonetheless, my aim is to show the cohesion of revivalism with marks one and six as bookends that will hopefully demonstrate that the temptations of revivalism haven't gone away.

MARK #1: REVERSE ENGINEERING

Revivalism at its core is the impulse to restore. In the first half of the nineteenth century, that meant men wanted to experience perpetually the movement of God that had occurred during the opening decades of the Great Awakening. Revivalism believes that humans can actually make this happen. As a result, preachers sought to re-create the conditions and results of spontaneous revival. The man most associated with this revivalism was Charles Finney.

Finney and other revivalists saw popular preachers (think Francis Asbury or Barton Stone), careful planning (Whitefield's use of print media), and emotional and physical manifestations (as in Edwards's *Religious Affections*) used to great effect for the conversion of souls. While he would never deny the necessity of grace, Finney taught that revival was not a miracle, but rather a work of man. It was the result of the right use of means. The means he practiced came to be known as the "new measures," and it included mass advertising, long revival meetings, naming unsaved people in public prayer, and, most infamously, the "anxious bench."

Finney's animating principle was that revival was the responsibility of Christians. God had ordained means and if the faithful would simply implement the tools given to them, then souls would be saved. Revival wasn't something divine and mysterious; instead, it could be actively engineered by studying past revivals, delineating their elements, and then putting those elements to work. Finney implemented his revivalism from upstate New York to Ohio. He left behind an influential legacy, even if most Christians today have never heard of him.

MARK #2: CELEBRITY CULTS OF PERSONALITY

Revivalism tends to revolve around well-known preachers, popular personalities, or even celebrities. This was not without precedent. People traveled by the thousands to hear Whitefield preach because it was Whitefield preaching. More people would likely have recognized Asbury than any of America's founding fathers.

But something changed with the transition to revivalism. Finney defended his new measures vigorously in the face of criticism and controversy. They became the essence of true revival in his mind, such that his ministry came to be identified with revivals. This meant that any warning, even from his friends, was perceived as a personal attack. He refused to heed any efforts to temper his methods. One contemporary, Elizabeth Brainerd, noted of his ministry, "At first all stood amazed and glorified God. At length persons of ill-balanced minds and scanty knowledge of Bible truth, began to glorify Mr. Finney. To them it was plain *he* had caused the revival, he had converted souls."

In his *Memoirs*, Finney himself made a revealing recollection. Remembering older ministers who were wary of his approach, he wrote, "Their opposition never made me ashamed, never convinced me that I was wrong in doctrine or practice, and I never made the slightest change in conducting revivals as a consequence of their opposition. I thought I was right. I still think so. I thought their opposition was impertinent and assuming, uncalled for and injurious to themselves and to the cause of God." As is often the case in revivalist ministries, there was a lack of accountability, an unwillingness to be corrected, and an equation of an individual with the work of God.

MARK #3: A RELIANCE ON HIGH PRODUCTION QUALITY

Revivalism is usually marked by a reliance on expertise and professionalism in the execution of the means of revival. Why the emphasis on excellence? Because if success depends on humans deploying the right means, then everything must be done just right. This was true in America with Finney's ministry, but also on the other side of the Atlantic.

The waning of spontaneous revivals and the move to arranged revivals took place in Britain in the 1840s. Finney's methods were met with enthusiasm by some, especially young pastors. Seasoned American evangelists, such as James Caughey, with their tried-and-true methods, toured the British Isles. A magazine, *The Revival*, was started by R. C. Morgan as a herald to further the efforts in 1859. Planned events became the norm, such that, when true revival broke out in the village of Hopeman, in Scotland, the newspaper there was compelled to clarify that what was being experienced was not contrived, publishing that "no attempts were made to 'get up' this movement."

MARK #4: EMOTIONAL MANIPULATION

Revivalism adopts strategies to promote emotion beyond preaching and prayer. This ranged in Finney's ministry from language intended to alarm to private meetings that pressured individuals to naming lost people in public prayer and even to directly addressing particular people from the pulpit. It's already been mentioned, but Finney's most notorious weapon was the "anxious seat."

There could be other physical gestures marking conversion, like standing, kneeling, or an altar call, but the anxious bench, also known as the "mourner's bench," was certainly the most dramatic. Here's how it worked: a bench or a number of seats were placed at the center of a gathering, in plain sight of the whole congregation adjacent to the pulpit. People would come to this section when they were ready to surrender to Christ. Once they arrived, they would receive intense prayer and exhortations. Those already converted would surround them. Often, there was singing, weeping, confession of sin, and physical manifestations of the Spirit. In Finney's words, the whole purpose of this exercise was that the unconverted be "brought right up to the single point of immediate submission."

MARK #5: REDUCTIONIST VIEWS OF CONVERSION

By way of summary, a dependence on all of the above betrays a view of conversion that falls woefully short of what Jesus calls being "born again." If revival comes as a result of human agency, then by implication regeneration must be explainable in similar terms. The issue is not the necessity of grace, but the primacy of grace. Is God sovereign in salvation or does he merely make salvation broadly available, while individuals ultimately determine their fate?

Nathaniel Taylor was a prestigious theologian who attempted to synthesize the ascendant Calvinism of his day with the revivalism of the Second Great Awakening. He was an ardent defender of the revivalism characteristic of Finney's preaching, which necessarily led to his altering of traditional Calvinism to the point that it was no longer recognizable. Though Taylor served as a Congregationalist minister and professor at Yale, he was accused of Arminianism and, worse, Pelagianism—and not without merit. Taylor denied the depravity of man, substitutionary atonement, and the sovereignty of God in preference of free will.

For Taylor and other advocates of revivalism, conversion really was up to the individual. Such decisions could be marked visibly by some outward gesture like kneeling or visiting the anxious bench. Conversion was not a supernatural imposition of grace, but the natural decision of anyone who truly understood the appeal of the Christian message and the Christian life.

MARK #6: INADEQUATE ECCLESIOLOGY

In revivalism, the publicized open-air preaching and the tent meetings replace the local church. By its very nature, revivalism looks beyond the ordinary means of grace. It means to go above and beyond, to transcend what God does in the day-to-day. In the end, all the marks we have looked at ultimately undervalue the power and centrality of ordinary local church ministry.

Revivalism raises a question: what community are individuals saved into? The excesses of the Second Great Awakening, specifically its ambivalence toward denominational forms, set the stage for undenominational evangelists like D. L. Moody and Ira Sankey. Ironically, the lack of regard for the local church in the mid-to-late nineteenth century promoted the promulgation of numerous denominations and radical sects that claimed to be the harbingers of true religion.

At the end of the day, conversion isn't the climax of the Christian life, but rather the start, the first step on the road to glorification. Along the way, however, we need more than a memory of an intense emotional moment. We need the local church. The local church is the community that affirms one's profession of faith at baptism and continues to affirm it through the Lord's Supper. The church provides the communal context for discipleship and sanctification.

CONCLUSION

That's an introduction to revivalism. In short, it persists on a host of wrong assumptions and faulty premises. Do you see any of these marks today?

What Can We Learn from Charles Spurgeon and the New York Revival of 1858?

By Geoff Chang

Something remarkable was happening in America in the spring of 1858. On September 23, 1857, Jeremiah C. Lanphier began holding weekly noontime prayer meetings at the North Reformed Dutch Church in New York. The first meeting had six in attendance. By the next week, the number grew to twenty. Then to forty. Lanphier soon changed the weekly gathering to a daily prayer meeting, and attendance continued to grow steadily, including both men and women. These meetings were marked by loud singing, short addresses, heartfelt sharing, and extemporaneous prayer.

By the following spring, the daily prayer meeting was so well attended that all three floors of the building were occupied. New prayer meetings sprouted up in other places throughout the city. As visitors to New York experienced this revival, they took that influence back to their hometowns, and these prayer meetings spread to other major cities, from Philadelphia to Kalamazoo. Newspapers throughout the English-speaking world reported on the stories of conversions and revival in America.[1] As Charles Spurgeon read these reports, he was encouraged. He compared this revival to the First Great Awakening that took place a hundred years ago under George Whitefield. "So marvelous—I had almost said, so miraculous—has been the sudden and instantaneous spread of religion throughout the great empire, that it is scarcely possible for us to believe the half of it, even though it should be told us."

But Spurgeon was not naïve when it came to revivals. He was often quite public in his criticisms against the revivalists of his day. In fact, he had such a reputation *against* revivalism that people were surprised to hear him speaking positively about the New York City revival. So, on March 28, 1858, Spurgeon preached his sermon, "The Great Revival."[2] The sermon reflects on the phenomenon of revival, and it presents Spurgeon's convictions about the work of God.

What did Spurgeon want his people to understand about God's work in revival?

GOD ALONE BRINGS ABOUT REVIVAL

First and foremost, the sermon shows that Spurgeon wanted his people to know that true revival comes from God alone. His sermon text was Isaiah 52:10. In this verse, the prophet describes God "as laying aside for awhile the garments of his dignity, and making bare his arm, that he may do his work in earnest, and accomplish his purpose for the establishment of his church." This is what happens during a revival.

Spurgeon observed that throughout church history, revival often came at unexpected times when God's people were declining and languishing

---

[1] For more on the New York Prayer Meeting Revival of 1858, see Talbot W. Chambers, *The New York City Noon Prayer Meeting: A Simple Prayer Gathering that Changed the World.* (Shippensburg, PA: Arsenal Press, 2019), Samuel Prime, *The Power of Prayer: The New York Revival of 1858.* (Edinburgh: Banner of Truth, 1998).

[2] All quotes come from Spurgeon's sermon, "The Great Revival," C. H. Spurgeon, *The New Park Street Pulpit: Containing Sermons Preached and Revised by the Rev. C. H. Spurgeon, Minister of the Chapel.* Vol. 4. (Pasadena, TX: Pilgrim Publications, 1975-1991), 161-168.

spiritually. In Spurgeon's words: "He finds a people hard and careless." But it is in these low times that God raises up preachers and stirs his people to pray so that the church is awakened. What explains this phenomenon? "The only real cause is his Spirit working in the minds of men."

This is why Spurgeon believed that there was no such thing as a revivalist. "Whenever I see a man who is called a revivalist, I always set him down for a cipher." Though some newspapers referred to Spurgeon as a revivalist, given the large crowds he attracted and his itinerant preaching, he always rejected the title. He insisted on simply being referred to as a pastor.

If God pleases to make use of a man for the promoting of a revival, well and good; but for any man to assume the title and office of a revivalist, and go about the country, believing that wherever he goes he is the vessel of mercy appointed to convey a revival of religion, is, I think, an assumption far too arrogant for any man who has the slightest degree of modesty.

Behind Spurgeon's rejection of revivalists was his foundational conviction that God alone brings revival. This belief in God's sovereign grace and man's absolute dependence shaped Spurgeon's entire philosophy of ministry. No matter how many sermons he preached, books he wrote, or institutions he founded, Spurgeon knew that he could never presume on the grace of God. All was in vain unless the Lord acted to save. The Christian's hope for any spiritual awakening must be in God's sovereign grace alone.

GOD USES PREACHING AND PRAYER TO BRING REVIVAL

While God is "the only actual cause" of revival, says the "Great Revival" sermon, God is pleased to use "instrumental causes" in his work. The main instrumental cause of revival "must be the bold, faithful, fearless preaching of the truth as it is in Jesus." Spurgeon observed how every generation experiences spiritual decline as gospel doctrines are modified, covered up, and dressed up in attractive errors so that, in the end, it is "in no way whatever related to the truth." But it's precisely in these moments that God raises up bold preachers who bring out the truth again. Whether Martin Luther, the Puritans, George Whitefield, or countless others, God has been pleased throughout church history to use faithful preachers of his Word to bring about revivals in the church.

But preaching isn't enough. The "earnest prayers of the church" must accompany the preaching of the Word. The most tireless ministries are in vain "unless the church waters the seed sown, with her abundant tears." This is what Spurgeon saw happening in America. "Every revival has been commenced and attended by a large amount of prayer. In the city of New York at the present moment, I believe there is not one single hour of the day, wherein Christians are not gathered together for prayer."

This was the lesson of the New York revival. While most other revivals in church history have been associated with a particular preacher, the New York revival displayed that God also works powerfully through congregational prayer. To be sure, preaching was still an essential part of these prayer meetings. But at the heart of the New York revival wasn't anyone's preaching, but countless Christians' constant prayers.

A REVIVAL'S RESULTS ARE ONLY TRULY SEEN IN THE LOCAL CHURCH

Revivalists believed that the Spirit's work showed up in sensational signs: shrieking, convulsions, falling, dancing, and more. Spurgeon believed such signs were the work of Satan, not of God. He warned his people:

Now, if you see any of these strange things arising, look out. There is that old Apollyon busy, trying to mar the work. Put such vagaries down as soon as you can, for where the Spirit works, he never works against his own precepts and his precept is, "Let all things be done decently and in order."

Revivalists also justified their meetings by reporting great numbers. Through innovative methods—like arranging for "decoy ducks" in the congregation to make public professions—revivalists could generate decisions for Christ. And they didn't hesitate to publish those results. Spurgeon continues: "It was only last week I saw a record of a certain place, in our own country, giving an account, that on such a day, under the preaching of the Rev. Mr. So-and-so, seventeen persons were thoroughly sanctified, twenty-eight were convinced of sin, and twenty-nine received the blessing of justification. ... All that I call farce!"

Why were such reports a farce? Because no revivalist could see into the heart. To count the number of people who were being sanctified, convicted of sin, or justified based on a mere profession was ridiculous. For Spurgeon, only one number mattered: those who joined the church. "We may easily say that so many were added to the church on a certain occasion, but to take a separate census of the convinced, the justified, and the sanctified, is absurd."

Only the church provided the accountability that made a profession of faith meaningful. A revival was like a miraculous spring pouring water out on the ground for all to drink. But apart from the church, that water would evaporate as soon as the spring closed. Through the church, however, that water could be caught in a container and maintained well beyond the life of the spring. Therefore, amid revival, Spurgeon urged pastors not to neglect the discipline of church membership:[3]

I must say, once more, that if God should send us a great revival of religion, it will be our duty not to relax the bonds of discipline. Some churches, when they increase very largely, are apt to take people into their number by wholesale, without due and proper examination. We ought to be just as strict in the paroxysms of a revival as in the cooler times of a gradual increase, and if the Lord sends his Spirit like a hurricane, it is ours to deal with skill with the sails lest the hurricane

---

3 For more on Spurgeon's practice of church membership, see: https://www.9marks.org/article/5-ways-spurgeons-metropolitan-tabernacle-cultivated-meaningful-membership/ and https://www.9marks.org/article/a-hedging-and-fencing-how-charles-spurgeon-promoted-meaningful-membership/

should wreck us by driving us upon some fell rock that may do us serious injury. Take care, ye that are officers in the church, when ye see the people stirred up, that ye exercise still a holy caution, lest the church become lowered in its standard of piety by the admission of persons not truly saved.

THE CHURCH IN EVERY GENERATION NEEDS REVIVAL

Many of Spurgeon's contemporaries thought the crying need of the church was better technology, dynamic preachers, bigger buildings, better finances, beautiful worship, efficient societies, or countless other church-growth ideas. But Spurgeon cut through that confusion and pinpointed the one need of every church in every generation: revival. The fundamental need of the church is for God to awaken preachers to the glories of the gospel, awaken Christians to holiness and prayer, convict sinners and bring them to saving faith in Christ, and raise up workers for the harvest.

Though Spurgeon had already experienced a revival under his ministry, he never got over longing for revival, and he urged his people to pray for an even greater blessing.

> Men, brethren and fathers, the Lord God hath sent us a blessing. One blessing is the earnest of many. Drops precede the April showers. The mercies which he has already bestowed upon us are but the forerunners and the preludes of something greater and better yet to come. He has given us the former; let us seek of him the latter rain, that his grace may be multiplied among us, and his glory may be increased.

CONCLUSION

Do you long for a revival in your church? In "The Great Revival," Spurgeon paints a picture of what a revival could look like. Can you imagine such a thing happening in your church? Wouldn't that be wonderful? Brothers and sisters, pray that God, in his mercy, would bring about such a revival.

Yet don't just listen to me talk about Spurgeon. Listen to Spurgeon himself:

> When there comes a revival, the minister all of a sudden finds that the usual forms and conventionalities of the pulpit are not exactly suitable to the times. He breaks through one hedge; then he finds himself in an awkward position, and he has to break through another. He finds himself perhaps on a Sunday morning, though a Doctor of Divinity, actually telling an anecdote—lowering the dignity of the pulpit by actually using a simile or metaphor—sometimes perhaps accidentally making his people smile, and what is also a great sin in these solid theologians, now and then dropping a tear. He does not exactly know how it is, but the people catch up to his words. "I must have something good for them," he says. He just burns that old lot of sermons; or he puts them under the bed, and gets some new ones, or gets none at all, but just gets his text, and begins to cry, "Men and brethren, believe on the Lord Jesus Christ, and you shall be saved."
>
> The old deacons say, "What is the matter with our minister?" The old ladies, who have heard him for many years and slept in the front of the gallery so regularly, begin to rouse, and say, "I wonder what has happened to him; how can it be? Why, he preaches like a man on fire. The tear runs over at his eye; his soul is full of love for souls." They cannot make it out; they have often said he was dull and dreary and drowsy. How is it all this is changed? Why, it is the revival. ...
>
> Well, then, directly after that the revival begins to touch the people at large. The congregation was once numbered by the empty seats, rather than by the full ones. But all of a sudden—the minister does not understand it—he finds the people coming to hear him. He never was popular, never hoped to be. All at once he wakes up and finds himself famous, so far as a large congregation can make him so. There are the people, and how they listen! They are all awake, all in earnest; they lean their heads forward, they put

their hands to their ears. His voice is feeble, they try to help him; they are doing anything so that they may hear the Word of Life.

And then the members of the church open their eyes and see the chapel full, and they say, "How has this come about? We ought to pray." A prayer-meeting is summoned. There had been five or six in the vestry: now there are five or six hundred, and they turn into the chapel. And oh! how they pray! That old stager, who used to pray for twenty minutes, finds it now convenient to confine himself to five; and that good old man, who always used to repeat the same form of prayer when he stood up, and talked about the horse that rushed into the battles and the oil from vessel to vessel, and all that, leaves all these things at home, and just prays, "O Lord, save sinners, for Jesus Christ's sake." And there are sobs and groans heard at the prayer meetings. It is evident that not one, but all, are praying; the whole mass seems moved to supplication. How is this again? Why, it is just the effect of the revival, for when the revival truly comes, the minister and the congregation and the church will receive good by it.

But it does not end here. The members of the church grow more solemn, more serious. Family duties are better attended to; the home circle is brought under better culture. Those who could not spare time for family prayer, find they can do so now, those who had no opportunity for teaching their children, now dare not go a day without doing it; for they hear that there are children converted in the Sunday school. There are twice as many in the Sunday school now as there used to be, and, what is wonderful, the little children meet together to pray, their little hearts are touched, and many of them show signs of a work of grace begun, and fathers and mothers think they must try what they can do for their families: if God is blessing little children, why should he not bless theirs?

And then, when you see the members of the church going up to the house of God, you mark with what a steady and sober air they go. Perhaps they talk on the way, but they talk of Jesus, and if they whisper together at the gates of the sanctuary, it is no longer idle gossip; it is no remark about, "How do you like the preacher? What did you think of him? Did you notice So-and-so?" Oh, no! "I pray the Lord that he might bless the word of his servant, that he might send an unction from on high, that the dying flame may be kindled, and that where there is life, it may be promoted and strengthened, and receive fresh vigor." This is their whole conversation.

And then comes the great result. There is an inquirers' meeting held: the good brother who presides over it is astonished, he never saw so many coming in his life before. "Why," says he, "there is a hundred, at least, come to confess what the Lord has done for their souls! Here are fifty come all at once to say that under such a sermon they were brought to the knowledge of the truth. Who hath begotten me these? How hath it come about? How can it be? Is not the Lord a great God that hath wrought such a work as this?" And then the converts who are thus brought into the church, if the revival continues, are very earnest ones. You never saw such a people. The outsiders call them fanatics. It is a blessed fanaticism. Others say, they are nothing but enthusiasts. It is a heavenly enthusiasm.

Everything that is done is done with such spirit. If they sing, it is like the crashing thunder; if they pray, it is like the swift, sharp dash of lightning, lighting up the darkness of the cold-hearted, and making them for a moment feel that there is something in prayer. When the minister preaches, he preaches like a Boanerges, and when the church is gathered together, it is with a hearty good will. When they give, they give with enlarged liberality; when they visit the sick, they do it with gentleness, meekness, and love. Everything is done with a single eye to God's glory; not of men, but by the power of God. Oh! that we might see such a revival as this!

But, blessed be God, it does not end here. The revival of the church then touches the rest of society. Men, who do not come forward and profess religion, are more punctual in attending the means of grace. Men that used to swear, give it up; they find it is not suitable for the times. Men that profaned the Sabbath, and that despised God, find it will not do; they give it all up. Times get changed; morality prevails; the lower ranks are affected. They buy a sermon where they used to buy some penny tract of nonsense.

The higher orders are also touched; they too are brought to hear the Word. Her ladyship, in her carriage, who never would have thought of going to so mean a place as a conventicle, does not now care where she goes so long as she is blessed. She wants to hear the truth, and a drayman pulls his horses up by the side of her ladyship's pair of grays, and they both go in and bend together before the throne of sovereign grace. All classes are affected. Even the senate feels it; the statesman himself is surprised at it, and wonders what all these things mean. Even the monarch on the throne feels she has become the monarch of a people better than she knew before, and that God is doing something in her realms past all her thought—that a great King is swaying a better scepter and exerting a better influence than even her excellent example.

Nor does it even end there. Heaven is filled. One by one the converts die, and it even gets fuller, the harps of heaven are louder, the songs of angels are inspired with new melody, for they rejoice to see the sons of men prostrate before the throne. The universe is made glad: it is God's own summer; it is the universal spring. The time of the singing of birds is come; the voice of the turtle is heard in our land. Oh! that God might send us such a revival of religion as this!

Finney with a Twist:

ELDER JACOB KNAPP AND THE ORIGINS OF BAPTIST REVIVALISM

By Caleb Morell

Synopsis: The methods of Charles Grandison Finney are well-documented. How his methods infiltrated Baptist churches is less-well known. In the 1830s and 40s, itinerant Baptist pastor Jacob Knapp adopted Finney's methods and travelled extensively spreading his revivalist methods among the Baptists. What emerged was "Finney with a Twist"—an amalgamation of Finney-ism specifically modified to the Baptist context. To Finney's protracted meetings, anxious bench, and anxious room, Knapp added two features that continue as standard-bearers of revivalism in Baptist churches today: spontaneous baptisms and child baptisms. Each of these innovations constituted a departure from Baptist norms and charted a course that continues to influence Baptist life today.

INTRODUCTION

Spontaneous baptisms have been all the rage in the SBC during the past decade. Since Elevation Church made headlines for baptizing people on the spot, the practice has had its share of supporters as well as detractors.[4] Today, many prominent SBC voices and churches commend the

---
4 "Megachurch Pastor Steven Furtick's 'Spontaneous Baptisms' Not so Spontaneous," *Religion*

practice, some even arguing that it's the key to reversing declining baptismal statistics and to foment revivals in our churches.[5] As baptisms have become more spontaneous, their subjects have grown younger and younger. At the Southern Baptist Convention in 2021, then-SBC Executive Committee President Ronnie Floyd called on churches to raise baptism statistics by lowering the age of the subject of baptisms.[6]

Whether you criticize such actions as novel or defend them as biblically warranted, it turns out they have an older pedigree than many expect. Both spontaneous baptisms and child baptisms find their modern origins in the work of a revivalist whose name is virtually unknown today: Elder Jacob Knapp (1799–1874).[7]

Knapp explicitly borrowed from Charles G. Finney to develop a uniquely Baptist form of revivalism, which can be fairly dubbed "Finney with a Twist." Alongside protracted meetings, anxious seats, and an insistence on an immediate decision, Knapp introduced two new features which shape Baptist life today: spontaneous baptisms and child baptisms. This article traces these six key aspects of Knapp's revivalism and how they were introduced into Baptist churches. By more clearly understanding the origins of these practices, pastors and congregants will have a better historical perspective for evaluating their consistency with Baptist polity and the teachings of Scripture.

News Service (blog), February 24, 2014, https://religionnews.com/2014/02/24/megachurch-pastor-steven-furticks-spontaneous-baptisms-spontaneous/.

5 "Long Hollow Revival Steeped in Prayer Sees 1,000 Baptisms since December | Baptist Press," https://www.baptistpress.com/, accessed May 6, 2022, https://www.baptistpress.com/resource-library/news/long-hollow-revival-steeped-in-prayer-sees-1000-baptisms-since-december/.

6 "Vision 2025 Amended, Adopted by Messengers | Baptist Press," https://www.baptistpress.com/, accessed May 6, 2022, https://www.baptistpress.com/resource-library/news/vision-2025-amended-adopted-by-messengers/.

7 While this article covers much of the same material as Iain Murray's excellent chapter on "The Baptists" in *Revival and Revivalism*, the primary source documents including Jacob Knapp's *Autobiography* and Charles G. Finney's work *Lectures on Revival* were each independently read by the author prior to reading Murray's chapter, with which the author is entirely in agreement.

INTRODUCING ELDER JACOB KNAPP

For many years, Elder Jacob Knapp was an ordinary pastor. He preached, counseled, encouraged, and shepherded a small congregation in upstate New York. But something was gnawing at Knapp that would not go away. While the Presbyterians had Finney, Knapp lamented that "there was no one man who stood forth as the champion and exemplar of revival measures" among the Baptists.[8] One day, Knapp felt God calling him to be that man.[9] So in 1833, Knapp quit his pastorate of eight years.

As he traveled from place to place, Knapp perfected Finney's techniques. He eventually published a complete record of his work and methods in his 1868 autobiography.[10] Once he hit the road, he was an immediate success. By 1840, Knapp was "almost as well-known as Finney."[11]

In fact, one contemporary claims that it was only through Knapp's influence that "Protracted meetings, as a system of measures, had acquired a permanent place" in the life of Baptist churches.[12] By the time of his death in 1874, Knapp claimed to have converted 100,000 persons at over 150 separate revivals.[13]

What were his methods and how did they become prominent in many Baptist churches?

THE INFLUENCE OF CHARLES G. FINNEY

Knapp was clearly influenced by Finney. In his autobiography, he wrote that around 1833 "the practice of holding protracted meetings began to enter in amongst the Baptist churches."[14] For Fin-

---

8 Jacob Knapp, *Autobiography of Elder Jacob Knapp* (Sheldon, 1868), 41.
9 Knapp, 41. "I felt that I was entering upon a path that had not been trodden before me."
10 Jacob Knapp, *Autobiography of Elder Jacob Knapp* (Sheldon, 1868).
11 William G. McLoughlin, *Modern Revivalism: Charles Grandison Finney to Billy Graham* (Wipf and Stock Publishers, 2004), 140. Cited in *Revival and Revivalism*, 312.
12 Knapp, xv.
13 McLoughlin, 140. Cited in *Revival and Revivalism*, 312.
14 Jacob Knapp, *Autobiography of Elder Jacob Knapp* (Sheldon, 1868), 28. As R. Jeffery writes, "the term [protracted meeting] is now generally used to designate... continuous exercises of preaching and prayer for several successive weeks, during which time the members of the church are urged to unusual exertions, in order to awaken the interest of the unconverted around them to the concerns of their everlasting well-being" (v). Another contemporary, David Benedict, writes, "At length protracted meetings began to be much talked of far and near, and so many

ney, their purpose was simply for people to "devote a series of days to religious services, in order to make a more powerful impression of divine things on the minds of the people."[15] An outside preacher would be brought in who agreed "to stay on the ground till the meeting is done," whether that meant days or weeks.[16] Between 1833 and 1874, Knapp led hundreds of such meetings, traveling from city to city, and preached nightly, sometimes for several weeks. But what made Finney and Knapp's meetings different from others was their use of "the anxious seat."

Knapp devotes a whole chapter to this in his autobiography: "The Utility of Anxious-Seats." He explains how at multiple points in the service he would give an invitation for the members of the audience to take their seats in the pews at the front of the room dubbed "the anxious bench" or "the anxious seat."[17] For Knapp, this was the key to a successful revival.[18] First, it challenged the sinner to take a stand. Second, it required a *public* committal, making it nearly impossible for the sinner to backtrack once he had taken the first step. As Knapp writes, "It is more dishonorable and more mortifying to go back than it is to go forward." Hence, "The more obstacles that can be put in the way of *receding* the better. ... All the barriers that can be put in the way of the anxious, to prevent their going back, should be piled

---

reports were circulated concerning the wonderful effects of them, that by many they were thought to be the very thing for promoting religious revivals… In process of time the Baptists became a good deal engaged in these peculiar gatherings, and many of them seemed much pleased with them. The revival ministers, as they were called, soon became very popular; they were sent for from far and near, and in many cases very large additions were made to our churches under their ministrations. But, in some cases, the old ministers and churches demurred… They were jealous of these wonder-working ministers in this business, and of a new machinery in the work of conversion…. To see converts coming into a church by wholesale was a pleasing idea to many members… But another class of members had fearful forebodings for the future" (David Benedict, *Fifty Years Among the Baptists* (Sheldon, 1860), 202-203).
15 Charles G. Finney, *Lectures on Revivals of Religion* (London: Thomas Tegg, 1839), 221.
16 Finney, 224.

17 By "the anxious seat," Finney referred to "the appointment of some particular seat in the place of meeting, where the anxious may come and be addressed particularly, and be made subjects of prayer, and sometimes conversed with individually" (Finney, 225).
18 Knapp, 43. Elsewhere Knapp writes, "After the sermon was finished… the anxious were invited forward…" (66).

up behind them."[19] Third, it was a convenient way of making a public acknowledgement of our need of Christ.[20] Fourth, the effect of seeing others go forward encouraged others to follow. "Thus," Knapp writes, "one can be the means of bringing others to a right decision by the force of example."[21] Fifth, by this means, ministers were able to immediately ascertain the success of their labors. All this and more can be accomplished by admonishing sinners to take specially designated seats in the front.

At the conclusion of the service, those seated in the "anxious seats," would follow Knapp to an "inquiry meeting," sometimes called the "anxious room."[22] (Knapp's critics called them the "finishing-off-room.")[23] At this meeting, Knapp focused less on giving "instructions to the anxious" and more on urging an "immediate decision—an instantaneous repentance, and faith in the Lord Jesus."[24] He writes, "I get all on their knees, and set them to crying to God (both saints and sinners), till he sends down salvation."[25]

Not unlike Finney, for Knapp the "anxious room" was a place to urge sinners to immediately profess faith in Christ. Whereas "thirty-five or forty years ago," Knapp wrote, "Baptists, Presbyterians, and Congregationalists would tell inquirers to go home, read their Bibles, reflect upon their condition, look within, dig deep, and be not deceived," Finney had introduced a more effective technique.[26] As Knapp reflected, such "methods of introspection" often result in conversion.[27] Instead, Knapp called for "an immediate surrender of their hearts to God" and insisted on "the exercise of faith and

---

19 Knapp, 214. Italics mine.
20 Knapp, 215.
21 Knapp, 215.
22 Knapp, 148. Finney called these "anxious meetings" (Finney, 221).
23 Knapp, 57.
24 Knapp, 221.
25 Knapp, 221. In another case he writes, "After I had concluded the preaching service, many of the unconverted, attracted by the voice of prayer, went into the anxious-room. Several of them fell on their knees and cried aloud for mercy. The converts began to plead with the anxious until all in the room were led to surrender their hearts to Christ" (61).
26 Knapp, 217.
27 Knapp, 217.

repentance on the spot" as a matter of obedience.[28]

BAPTIZING FINNEY'S REVIVALISM

So far none of Knapp's methods could be described as novel. But in 1840, Knapp introduced spontaneous baptisms and child baptisms.

While ministering in New York City in 1840, at the Baptist Tabernacle in Mulberry Street, Knapp began practicing what he called "instantaneous baptisms."[29] While Knapp was meeting with "the anxious" upstairs, the church was examining candidates for membership downstairs and baptizing them on the spot. Knapp writes, "As fast as [they] found peace in believing with all their hearts, I sent them below to present themselves to the church."[30] In fact, at one point, the deacons even complained to Knapp that he was "sending the converts faster than the church could receive them."[31]

Knapp acknowledged that "instantaneous baptisms" were contrary to Baptist practice and history. According to Knapp, Baptists in his day "were opposed to sudden conversions," saying that "the seed must have time to germinate."[32] But Knapp thought it ridiculous to require "converts [to] come before a committee and wait a month before they could be baptized."[33] Not only was this process slow, it seemed grounded in sinful suspicion. "It seemed to be taken for granted," Knapp writes, "that every applicant at the doors of the church must be either a hypocrite or the victim of self-delusion."[34] Such tedious processes unnecessarily "retard a revival," whereas the instantaneous baptism of converts puts wind in its sails.[35]

Moreover, Knapp brought Scripture to bear in opposition to delay, citing the Book of Acts in

---

28 Knapp, 217-218.
29 Knapp, 210.
30 Knapp, 108.
31 Knapp, 108. During another series of meetings in Canton, IL in 1851, where they baptized seventy persons in one week, Knapp writes, "It was our custom to follow close upon the heels of the apostles in the baptizing of converts. When one rose up, rejoicing in the blessed Savior, the church would vote him right in, and we baptized him" (166).
32 Knapp, 43.
33 Knapp, 108.
34 Knapp, 44.
35 Knapp, 211.

support. After all, he argues, in Acts 2, 3000 were baptized "the same day," and the Philippian jailer was baptized not only the same night of his conversion, but "the same hour" (Acts 16:33).[36] The case of Saul of Tarsus," he argues, "is the only one recorded in the New Testament of a person whose baptism was delayed after conversion," being baptized three days later.[37] As Knapp concludes, "The apostles understood the [Great] commission to require of them the instantaneous baptism of all who professed their faith in Christ."[38] And again: "The New Testament makes no provision of a moment's delay between the exercise of faith and the act of baptism."[39]

Knapp's innovations aside, it is worth noting that his "instantaneous baptisms" still required the approval of the congregation, and invariably led directly to uniting with that church in membership. In other words, despite their immediacy, even Knapp recognized the necessity of the congregational examination of a candidate prior to baptism *and* the inseparable link between baptism and church membership.

At the same time, Knapp's bar for membership and baptism was far short of the rigorous examinations which were common in Baptist churches in the mid-nineteenth century. Instead of probing questions and assessing for fruit of conversion, Knapp urges a "mere profession" bar for baptism and membership. He writes,

It is very evident that the apostles in no instance demanded of a candidate a probationary trial, nor even a metaphysical analysis of the workings of their minds under conviction, as prerequisites of baptism. They simply required a sincere expression of repentance of sin and faith in Jesus Christ.[40]

And adopting such a bar for baptism leads straight into Knapp's

---

36 Knapp, 208. For a response to arguments of this kind and an assessment of the baptisms in the Book of Acts, see Caleb Morell, "Does the Book of Acts Teach Spontaneous Baptisms?," 9Marks, accessed January 6, 2022, https://www.9marks.org/article/does-the-book-of-acts-teach-spontaneous-baptisms/
37 Knapp, 209.
38 Knapp, 210.
39 Knapp, 222.
40 Knapp, 209.

second innovation in Baptist history: baptizing children.

An examination of baptismal ages among Baptists in America from 1700–1840, shows that the most common age for baptism was 19.[41] In fact, the few instances where the baptismal candidate was 12 or 13 were treated as exceptional cases. By the 1880s, this had flipped entirely. At this point, 12 or 13 was the norm; 19 became the exception.[42] At some point, in the mid-nineteenth century a shift occurred in Baptist churches, much of which can be attributed to Knapp.

Having lowered the bar for baptism to a "mere profession" without examination of fruit, Knapp cannot help but open the door for the baptism of children. He admits this himself, "A child who is old enough to repent and believe is not too young to be baptized."[43] And Knapp practiced what he preached. In February 1867, at the Central Baptist Church in Trenton, NJ, seventeen children belonging to the Sunday School were baptized.[44] The following Sunday, seventy more children joined the church, largely due, in Knapp's mind, to the moral influence of the children who had been baptized the Sunday previously.[45]

CONCLUSION

There's no question that revivalism is alive and well in Baptist churches today. What William G. McCloughlin wrote about revivalism being "the national religion in the United States" in the nineteenth century could doubtless be said of today.[46] Knapp's adaptation of and expansion upon Finney's "new measures" had lasting implications on the religious life and practices of Baptists in America.

Pastors need to understand that a change occurred among American Baptists in the nineteenth century, one that continues apace to this day. This change

---

41 Caleb Morell, "Too Young to Dunk? An Examination of Baptists and Baptismal Ages, 1700–1840," 9Marks, accessed January 5, 2022, https://www.9marks.org/article/too-young-to-dunk-an-examination-of-baptists-and-baptismal-ages-1700-1840/.
42 This observation is based on the author's study of baptismal ages at Metropolitan Baptist Church, 1884-1888.
43 Knapp, 213.
44 Knapp, 187.
45 Knapp, 188.
46 McLoughlin, *Modern Revivalism*, 66. Cited in *Revival and Revivalism*, 277.

has shaped our intuitions about conversion, membership, baptism, and what it means to practice regenerate church membership. We live in a world infused with revivalistic intuitions and institutional practices that unintentionally undermine what it even means to be a Baptist church. By understanding the historical roots of revivalism, pastors will be better equipped to critically assess practices often taken for granted today.

Edwards, Revival, and the Necessary Means of Prayer

By Mark Rogers

Jonathan Edwards was part of an extraordinary revival in the 1730s and 1740s. Few Christians would argue that the First Great Awakening was the result of manufactured or manipulated revivalism. But what many have missed is that before revival visited Edwards' church and nation, Edwards sought it. He longed for it and prayed for it, and when it came he urged others to fan its flames through the use of certain means.

My claim will come as a surprise to those who have seen the First Great Awakening as a series of revivals in which "the instruments are not apparent," but "seemed to come directly from the presence of the Lord, unasked for, unexpected."[47] For decades, historians and pastors have contrasted the First and Second Great Awakenings in part by claiming that the leaders of 19th century revivalism used means to pursue revival, while Edwards and his 18th century colleagues did not. This common narrative obscures the fact that Edwards called for a vigorous

---

47 Calvin Colton, *History and Character of American Revivals of Religion* (London: F. Westley and A.H. Davis, 1832), 5–6; qtd. affirmingly in David Kling, *Field of Divine Wonders*, 239.

use of what he saw as biblical means for the explicit purpose of seeing God send an extraordinary revival.

Edwards steadfastly believed that revival was a work of God, not man: "There is very much to convince us, that God alone can bestow it, and show our entire and absolute dependence on him for it. The insufficiency of human abilities to bring to pass any such happy change in the world . . . does now remarkably appear."[48] Nevertheless God also has ordained that his people use the means he has given to them to bring this great work about. Revival is not a gift of God apart from human instrumentality, Edwards argued, but a work "accomplished by means."[49] Therefore, it was the duty of all to do their "utmost in the place that God has set them in, to promote it."[50] Edwards did not wait passively while God sent a revival that came unexpectedly and unasked for. Edwards believed the Bible, and especially biblical prophecy, pointed to three specific means that would be a part of major revivals God would send: (1) spreading the news of God's work, (2) the preaching of the truth, and (3) united prayer. This article will focus on Edwards' call to united prayer, and some of the impact it had among those who heeded his call.

AN HUMBLE ATTEMPT

In 1743, as the Great Awakening was still sweeping through the colonies, Edwards wrote *Some Thoughts Concerning the Present Revival of Religion in New England* (1743). In Part V, he encouraged ministers to get together and pray for the growth and spread of the revivals.[51] Edwards' proposal

---

48 Jonathan Edwards, *A History of the Work of Redemption*, ed. John F. Wilson, vol. 9 of *The Works of Jonathan Edwards* (New Haven: Yale University Press, 1989), 359.
49 Ibid., 9:458-459.
50 Jonathan Edwards, *Apocalyptic Writings*, ed. Stephen J. Stein, vol. 5 in *The Works of Jonathan Edwards* (New Haven: Yale University Press, 1977), 395-396, 383.

51 "I have often thought it would be a thing very desirable, and very likely to be followed with a great blessing, if there could be some contrivance that there should be an agreement of all God's people in America, that are well affected to this work, to keep a day of fasting and prayer to God; wherein we should all unite on the same day in humbling ourselves before God for our past long continued lukewarmness and unprofitableness ... and that he would continue and still carry on this work, and more abundantly and extensively pour out his Spirit; and particularly that he would pour out his Spirit upon ministers; and

bore fruit in October 1744 when a group of Scottish pastors met to plan a quarterly concert of prayer. Edwards heard about it from his Scottish friends at the end of 1745 and was thrilled. He led his congregation to participate in the concert of prayer, and in 1747 he published *An Humble Attempt to Promote Explicit Agreement and Visible Union of God's People in Extraordinary Prayer For the Revival of Religion and the Advancement of Christ's Kingdom on Earth, pursuant to Scripture-promises and Prophecies concerning the Last Time*.[52]

Edwards' purpose in writing *An Humble Attempt* was to publicize the Scottish concert of prayer, and to urge readers to participate. The book offers a thoroughly biblical argument.

He repeatedly makes the connection between the prayers of God's people and the blessing of revival: "The prophets, in their prophecies of the restoration and advancement of the church, very often speak of it as what shall be done in answer to the prayers of God's people." And again: "The Scriptures give us great reason to think, that when once there comes to appear much of a *spirit of prayer* in the church of God for this mercy, then it will soon be accomplished."[53]

"THE EXTRAORDINARY PRAYERS OF HIS PEOPLE"

Edwards was convinced from Scripture that God would send revival as an answer to the prayers of his people. Therefore, he labored to promote a widespread movement of prayer. While Edwards published and organized, he did not think God had left it in human hands to work or program this prayer movement. Edwards explained, "From the representation made in the prophecy … it will be fulfilled something after

---

that he would bow the heavens and come down (II Sam. 22:10; Ps. 18:9), and erect his glorious kingdom through the earth…. some considerable number of ministers might meet together and draw up the proposal, wherein a certain day should be pitched upon …. In such a way, perhaps, might be fulfilled in some measure such a general mourning and supplication of God's people as is spoken of, Zech. 12, at the latter end, with which the church's glorious day is to be introduced." Edwards, *The Great Awakening*, 4:520-521.

52 Edwards, *Apocalyptic Writings*, 5:308-437.

53 Edwards, *The Great Awakening*, 4:350, 353.

this manner; first, that there shall be given much of a spirit of prayer to God's people, in many places disposing them to come into an express agreement, unitedly to pray to God in an extraordinary manner." People were not first in the process, God was. Of course, he gave the desire to pray first, or the people would never possess it. The prayers would be extraordinary, but that's because God would make it so. Edwards explained, "It is God's will, through his wonderful grace, that the prayers of his saints should be one great and principal means of carrying on the designs of Christ's kingdom in the world. When God has something very great to accomplish for his church, 'tis his will that there should precede it the extraordinary prayers of his people."[54] In other words, the Bible says revival will follow "extraordinary prayers." Therefore, people should gather and pray for revival.

PEOPLE PRAYED

Edwards' *An Humble Attempt* did not receive wide circulation or lead to a widespread prayer movement in the late 1740s or 50s. But nearly forty years after its publication (1784), a Scottish pastor sent a copy of Edwards' book to some Baptist leaders in England, including Andrew Fuller, John Ryland, and John Sutcliffe. They republished the book and urged churches to begin meeting the first Monday of each month to pray for revival. Within a few years, those particular Baptists would act on their prayers for worldwide revival by sending William Carey to India as a missionary and launching the modern missions movement.

On the American side, a close-knit group of Edwardsian, Congregational pastors republished *An Humble Attempt* in 1794. They also began to heed its call. Connecticut ministers called for a quarterly concert of prayer for revival. A group met in Lebanon, Connecticut in 1794 and committed to begin praying the first Tuesday of each quarter. These ministers also sent out circular letters and started a correspondence committee to promote prayer for revival.[55] In October 1794, prompted

---

54 Edwards, *The Great Awakening*, 4:516.

55 Conforti, *Jonathan Edwards, Religious*

by a letter from Walter King, of Norwich, Connecticut, the Hartford North Association committed to meet every other Wednesday for prayer. They sent letters urging larger denominational bodies to do the same.[56] In June 1795, the General Association of Connecticut adopted a resolution on seasons of prayer for revival.[57] Altogether, two thirds of Connecticut churches adopted the concert of prayer. For example, the Tolland County Association passed the following resolution in October 1795: "That this Association being anxiously impressed with the apparent decline of religion, unanimously agree to meet on the second Tuesday of each month, beginning with next November, for the purpose of special prayer for the outpouring of the Holy Spirit, and for other religious exercises."[58]

New England Congregationalists weren't the only Americans gathering to pray in the 1790s. In late 1794, Baptist ministers in New England, including Isaac Backus and Stephen Gano, sent a circular letter encouraging ministers and churches of all denominations to pray for revival. They borrowed directly from Edwards' lengthy book title, exhorting believers to "carry into execution the humble attempt to promote explicit agreement and visible union of God's people in extraordinary prayer for the revival of religion and the advancement of Christ's kingdom on earth." The letter suggested setting aside the first Tuesday in January of 1795 and once a quarter thereafter "until the good Providence of God prospering our endeavors, we shall obtain the blessing for which we pray." Pastors and churches all over America, including Methodists and Presbyterians, Baptists, and Congregationalists, began meeting to pray for revival. Some quarterly, some monthly, and some weekly.

GOD ANSWERED

Those many prayer meetings were followed, in many cases, by

Tradition & American Culture, 16.
56 Kling, *Field of Divine Wonders*, 62-64.
57 *The Records of the General Association of Ye Colony of Connecticut: Begun June 20th, 1738; Ending June 19th, 1799* (Hartford, CT: Case, Lockwood & Brainard, 1888), 163.
58 Charles Roy Keller, *The Second Great Awakening in Connecticut* (New Haven, CT: Yale University Press, 1942), 50.

revivals. Real, biblical, God-sent revival didn't go away after the First Great Awakening. By 1800, Isaac Backus was rejoicing: "The revivals of religion in different parts of our land have been wonderful." For example, the rapid growth of united prayer in Connecticut in the 1790s was followed by a remarkable revival among those same churches between 1798 and 1800. Members were convicted of sin, churches experienced God's presence and power in extraordinary ways, and hundreds of new converts were added to the church. Those stories need to be recovered and retold. But for the purpose of this article, it's enough to note that in nearly every case, the revivals in those local churches were preceded by and began with united prayer.

For example, Joseph Washburn reported that a revival began in Farmington in February 1799 "in a disposition to unite in prayer for the divine presence, and a revival of religion." They soon agreed to meet "at least once a fortnight . . . for the purpose of special united prayer for a revival of religion."[59] Reverend William F. Miller of Windsor saw revival soon after he appointed a weekly meeting that was successful "in bringing many people together to unite in prayer to God, and in seeking the precious blessings of his grace."[60] Reverend Ammi Robbins reported that a revival began at Norfolk in January 1799, after five years of quarterly concerts of prayer.[61] Through many revival accounts found in the *Connecticut Evangelical Magazine*, fervent and united prayer for revival is a common theme. A January 1802 article urged readers to continue to "form Concerts of prayer," since they "are things highly becoming the church of a prayer-hearing God," and "an all-important means in advancing the kingdom of the Redeemer." The author wrote that the effectiveness of united prayer "is set in a clear point of light" in President Edwards' *Humble Attempt* and

---

[59] *Connecticut Evangelical Magazine* 1 (April 1801): 379-380.
[60] *Connecticut Evangelical Magazine* 1 (January 1801): 269.
[61] *Connecticut Evangelical Magazine* 1 (February 1801): 312.

declared, "Every Christian ought to read this book."[62]

APPLICATION

Whether you read Edwards' *Humble Attempt* or not, I hope you are encouraged to apply his main point. God can and does work in extraordinary ways, and the Bible teaches that God works in response to fervent, united prayer. Therefore, we should regularly meet together and pray for God to revive his people and save the lost. The history of real revival in America should encourage us to continue (or start) holding prayer meetings in our churches. It should also encourage pastors to gather with each other for united prayer. We know we cannot manufacture revival. But we should be just as convinced that God can send it.

So why not gather with a few other pastors in your area once a month or once per quarter to pray for God to send revival? He has answered those kinds of prayers before.

---

[62] *Connecticut Evangelical Magazine 2* (January 1802): 269.

Revival Comes to Washington

By Caleb Morell

Synopsis: In 1876, Washington churches partnered together to host a 105-day-long revival meeting in the National Capital. This event illustrates the extent to which modern revivalism impacted American evangelicalism and provides a broader backdrop for many of the revivalistic methods we continue to see practiced today.

In the nineteenth century, revivals ceased to be regarded as the spontaneous work of the Holy Spirit and instead became planned events: the result of intercessory prayer, careful planning, and meticulous execution. As Iain Murray notes with irony, "Instead of being 'surprising' [revivals] might now be even announced in advance."[63] The difference between the older reliance on the ordinary means of grace and the newer reliance on ever-changing methods has been aptly described as the difference between "revival and revivalism."[64]

This article examines one instance of "revivalism" in 1876—when the churches of Washington, D.C. partnered together to bring a world-famous revivalist to the National Capital for a hundred-day-long series of protracted meetings. I will examine four features of this Washington revival—partnership, prayer, press, and preaching—before offering three concluding reflections that attempt to bridge the gap between past practices and present realities.

It would be simplistic to label this event either "good" or "bad." Like all imperfect efforts, the good and bad are mixed. Instead of rendering a conclusive verdict, this article simply records, analyzes, and observes how much of the present obsession with numbers, decisions, and new methods finds its roots in nineteenth-century revivalism.

PARTNERSHIP

Between 1875 and 1876, five Washington pastors came together to pray for revival.[65] They represented the various Protestant denominations of the city: Congregational, Presbyterian, Baptist, Methodist, and Lutheran. Together,

---

63 Iain Hamish Murray, *Revival and Revivalism: The Making and Marring of American Evangelicalism 1750-1858* (Banner of Truth Trust, 1994), xviii.

64 Iain Hamish Murray, *Revival and Revivalism: The Making and Marring of American Evangelicalism 1750-1858* (Banner of Truth Trust, 1994).

65 According to Dr. Rankin, of First Congregational Church, these were Dr. Mason Noble of Sixth Presbyterian Church, Dr. E. H. Gray of Fourteenth Street Baptist Church, Dr. S. Domer of St. Paul's English Lutheran Church. Rankin does not name the fifth, but it seems likely that it was William S. Hammond of the Ninth-Street Methodist Protestant Church (Everett O. Alldredge, "Centennial History of First Church 1865-1965," n.d., https://www.firstuccdc.org/wp-content/uploads/2021/03/fccucc-centennial-history1.pdf).

they formed the "Union Revival Committee" in order to organize a revival in the Capital.⁶⁶ They secured the services of Edward Payson Hammond and his accompanying musician William W. Bentley of New York, who agreed to spend the spring of 1876 in Washington.⁶⁷

Figure 2: A sketch of Edward Payson Hammond from his biography 'The Reaper and the Harvest'⁶⁸

66 As the *National Republican* explained, "A general committee of arrangements was appointed, consisting of Rev. Drs. Cleveland, Rankin, Gray, Noble, Domer, B.P. Brown, W.S. Hammond, Messrs. J.C. Harkness, Wm. Stickney, F.L. Moore, President Gallaudet, C.H. Merwin, F.H. Smith, Warren Choate, A.T. Steward, Dr. Presbery, S.S. Bryant, and B.H. Steinmetz" (*National Republican*, 2 Feb 1876, Page 4).
67 Bentley was described by the *National Republican* as "a musician with considerable reputation for efficiency in singing the Gospel" (*National Republican*, 2 February 1876, Page 4).
68 *The Reaper and the Harvest: Or, Scenes and Incidents in Connection with the Work of the Holy Spirit in the Life and Labors of Rev. Edward Payson Hammond, M.A.* (Funk & Wagnalls, 1884).

PRAYER

As the churches awaited Hammond's arrival, they began to gather daily for prayer. At these midday prayer meetings—similar to the famous New York prayer revival—attendees were encouraged to write down or publicly share prayer requests. Each prayer request was read aloud and recorded simply: "a father for his two sons," "for a man and wife who have not been to church for nine years," "for a backslider who is not satisfied," "for a man who wants to be a Christian, but his wife is his hindrance," "for an unconverted mother and father," etc.⁶⁹ These daily prayer meetings, which had begun long before Hammond's arrival and continued long after his departure, constituted the core of the revival in Washington.

PRESS

Like other revivalists, Hammond depended heavily on friendly press.⁷⁰ While he "could only speak

69 *National Republican*, 19 May 1876, Page 4.
70 In her study of revivals in the United States, Kathryn Long found that "newspapers played a major part in shaping the images of most, if not all, the well-known revivalists after 1858."

to hundreds, the secular papers could speak to thousands."[71] Moreover, like a self-fulfilling prophecy, the more the Press touted the revival's success, the greater the crowds that would be drawn out of curiosity. As his biographer explained, "The best way to promote revivals of religion is to tell of them in other places."[72]

As a result, Hammond kept meticulous records so as to always be ready to cite his successes to the press. One of his innovations was to ask every person who came forward to the inquiry meeting to sign a "covenant card," which stated, "I, the undersigned, hope I have found Jesus to be my precious Savior; and I promise, with his help, to live as his loving child and faithful servant all my life." While this card was kept by the signer, their name was recorded in Hammond's book to keep track of the number of converts.[73]

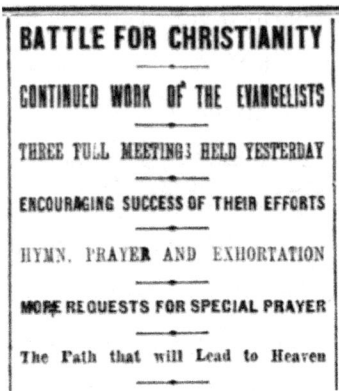

Figure 3: *National Republican*, 19 Feb 1876, page 4

PREACHING

The revival meetings formally commenced on Saturday, February 5, 1876, at St. Paul's English Lutheran Church in Washington, DC.[74] The locations for the meetings shifted as various churches made their buildings available. Two to three meetings were held daily, each consisting of Bible reading, exposition, prayer, and testimony. During the main meetings in the evening, Hammond would

---

Kathryn Teresa Long, *The Revival of 1857-58: Interpreting an American Religious Awakening* (Oxford University Press, 1998), 29.
71 *National Republican*, 10 Feb 1876, Page 4.
72 *The reaper & the harvest*, vii.
73 McCloughlin, *Modern Revivalism*, 157.

74 It is unfortunate that the biography of E.P. Hammond by Phineas C. Headley omits his time in Washington, only stating that "several years, including that in which he labored in Washington, D.C., have been omitted almost entirely. At some future time, it is hoped, another book will be written, giving an account of these harvest scenes." Phineas Camp Headley, *The Reaper and the Harvest: Or, Scenes and Incidents in Connection with the Work of the Holy Spirit in the Life and Labors of Rev. Edward Payson Hammond, M.A.* (Funk & Wagnalls, 1884), 537.

preach an evangelistic sermon, which included a gospel presentation and a call to response.⁷⁵

But Hammond's gospel presentation often contained strong notes of moral reform and self-improvement. For instance, in his message on Sunday April 2, 1876, to an overflowing crowd at First Congregational Church, Hammond chose Amos 6:1 for his text, "Woe to those who are at ease in Zion." His message focused largely on the moral plight of society and the need for personal transformation. "If you go through the saloons and hotels and offices of this city and listen to men who are not Christians talking," he decried, "you will hear God's moral law being attacked, and his infinite power and wisdom called into question. And yet, you say, this is none of our business." At the conclusion, "the different classes present were invited to rise for prayers," and "nearly all arose by an involuntary impulse."⁷⁶

By decrying public and private wickedness and identifying Christ as the only solution, Hammond risked falling into preaching a message of moral transformation. While he presented Christ as the only way to personal salvation, the balance of Hammond's preaching focused on broad social reform: society was falling apart and only personal salvation could ensure the morality needed to prevent further decay.⁷⁷

---

75 According to the *National Republican*, the gospel, as preached by Hammond, was as follows: "Jesus, the son of God, created this beautiful world we live in. The laws that God devised for the government of his children were broken by them, and they came under a penalty for their transgression. Jesus then stepped forth and offered to pay the penalty by his sufferings and death. He came down into this world, took upon himself the nature of ward, and died that we might live. He was forsaken by his father, that we might not be forsaken. He was treated as a sinner that we might be freed from the penalty of our transgressions. He died and ascended into heaven. But he will come again to earth and judge all, and separate the good from the evil, the righteous from the wicked."

76 *National Republican*, 3 Apr 1876, Page 1.
77 In his study, *Revivalism and Cultural Change*, George M. Thomas has found that the prevalence of revivalism corresponded with greater support for the Republican and Prohibition parties. He offers the interpretation that religious movements, like those of the 'Second Great Awakening,' "articulate a new moral order and that each attempts to have its version of that order dominate the moral-political universe." See George M. Thomas, *Revivalism and Cultural Change: Christianity, Nation Building, and the Market in the Nineteenth-Century United States* (University of Chicago Press, 2019), 2.

ASSESSING THE FRUIT

Approximately 285 official revival meetings were held in Washington, D.C. between February 5, 1876, and May 20, 1876—a span of 105 days. Ever the prodigious record-keeper, Hammond claimed to have converted 1,900 in Washington,[78] the majority of which were children under sixteen.[79] If this number is accurate, and Washington's population was around 150,000 in 1876,[80] then somewhere around 1 in 78, or 1.3 percent of Washington's residents were claimed by Hammond as "converts" during his revival.

But long after Hammond had moved on to the next city, Washington pastors and churches dealt with the fallout and consequences of the revival. What implications did revivalism have on pastoral ministry in the nation's capital?

---

[78] The New York Daily Herald reported "over 2,000 converts" (See *New York Daily Herald*, 03 Sep 1876, Page 4).
[79] McLoughlin, *Modern Revivalism*, 156-157.
[80] "District of Columbia Population History," *Washington DC History Resources* (blog), August 30, 2014, https://matthewbgilmore.wordpress.com/district-of-columbia-population-history/.

1. *Pressure to adopt new methods*

The "new measures" of revivalism created distinct pressures for pastors to follow suit or fall behind. If a church refused to participate in the revival, they were unlikely to reap any of its "fruits." Revivals presented an opportunity to hear new preachers, attend new churches, and frequently led to changes in membership from one denomination or church to another.

Of course, not all of Washington churches participated. And those who failed to play along lost the most. Pastors felt a new pressure to grow the church through revivals or risk falling behind. In the long run, this undermined the slow, patient work of pastoring.

2. *Dependence on new measures for church growth*

A second consequence of the growing revivalism was a reliance on new methods for bringing in new members. Rather than spontaneous professions of faith over the course of the year, revival services were increasingly seen as the proper place for professions of faith. For example, between 1884 and 1888, 91 percent of all professions of faith at Metropolitan Baptist Church occurred during protracted meetings. If a pastor wanted to grow his church, build a larger building, or expand to a new neighborhood, the universally agreed upon course of action was simple: host a revival.

3. Justification by numbers

A third consequence was an increased reliance on numbers as the barometer of success. When Payson concluded the revival in Washington, he complained that the work had begun slowly, and the meetings had not been as crowded as he had hoped.[81] But Washington pastors were pleased by the increases in membership they saw in their churches as a result of the revival. First Congregational Church reported that they had added 170 members during Hammond's campaign, including 115 on a single Lord's Day.[82] Calvary Baptist saw their church membership increase from 381 to 505.[83]

But these short-term additions masked long-term challenges. For instance, in a study of New York revivals, historian Curtis Johnson found that members who joined churches during revivals, on average, were excommunicated at a faster and higher rate than members who joined outside of revival services.[84] At Metropolitan Baptist Church, which continued the revivalistic practices throughout the 1880s, 45 percent of members baptized during revival meetings between 1884 and 1888 were eventually dropped from membership because they had stopped attending services.

---

81 *Evening Star*, 23 Nov 1876, Page 4.
82 Everett O. Alldredge, *Centennial History of First Congregational Church 1865-1965*, p. 28-29. https://www.firstuccdc.org/wp-content/uploads/2021/03/fccucc-centennial-history1.pdf. This number is confirmed by the *National Republican*, which wrote on May 9, 1876, "Large accessions to the various churches were made on that Sabbath—over one hundred uniting with one of the churches" (*National Republican*, 09 May 1876, Page 4).
83 Tiller, *At Calvary*, p. 16.
84 Curtis D. Johnson, "The Protracted Meeting Myth: Awakenings, Revivals, and New York State Baptists, 1789–1850." *Journal of the Early Republic* 34, no. 3 (2014): 355. http://www.jstor.org/stable/24486904.

CONCLUSION

The Washington revival of 1876 gives a vivid picture of the extent to which modern revivalism impacted and infiltrated American evangelicalism. As churches across many denominations bought into revivalism's promises and adopted revivalism's methods, they stopped looking for long-term indicators of success, such as perseverance and spiritual growth. Instead, they were after something else: a boost in membership that would validate the effectiveness of their ministry.

Sadly, such short-term perspectives often neglected long-term concerns. The same is true today. As we consider the mixed fruit of modern evangelicalism, pastors need to understand that the origin of many of our practices can be traced back to the revivalism of the nineteenth century.

Forgotten, Real Revivals of the Second Great Awakening

By Mark Rogers

After revival swept through his congregation in the winter of 1807 and 08, adding over 200 members to his church, Edward Dorr Griffin wrote to his friend, Ashbel Green. He described the revival as follows:

This work, in point of power and stillness, exceeds all that I have ever seen. While it bears down everything with irresistible force, and seems almost to dispense with human instrumentality, it moves with so much silence. … The converts are strongly marked with humility and self-distrust: instead of being elated with confident hopes, they are inclined to tremble. Many of them possess deep and discriminating views; and all, or almost all, are born into the distinguishing doctrines of grace.[85]

---
[85] William Buell Sprague, *Memoir of the Rev. Edward D. Griffin, D.D., Compiled Chiefly from His Own Writings* (Albany, NY: Packard, Van Benthuysen & Co., 1838), 93.

Characterized by "stillness," "silence," and the "distinguishing doctrines of grace," this revival may seem out of place in the period known as the Second Great Awakening. Many see the First Great Awakening as controlled, orderly, robustly theological, and Calvinistic, epitomized by the theology and leadership of Jonathan Edwards; conversely, the Second Great Awakening is viewed as emotional, wild, atheological, and Arminian, epitomized by frenzied camp meetings on the frontier or Charles Finney's manipulative "new measures." The First is seen as a genuine work of God, while the Second is described as a work of man-centered manipulation. The First is seen as revival, while the second as revivalism. These sharp contrasts fit when focusing on certain aspects of each era. But these generalizations neglect large and important spheres of the Second Great Awakening. By naming the entire movement a result of man-made revivalism, we fail to recognize many examples of true revival between 1798 and 1820 that we can rejoice in and learn from.

This article will describe some revivals of the Second Great Awakening that we have largely forgotten. I focus on the earliest years of the Awakening, but these revivals are characteristic of many similar revivals that took place in New England, New Jersey, and New York between 1798 and 1820 among disciples of Jonathan Edwards. I hope these stories will encourage, I hope they will increase our desire for revival, and I hope they will help us to stop saying, in an unqualified way, that the Second Great Awakening was a result of man-made revivalism.

THE BEGINNING OF THE AWAKENING

Griffin was mentored by Jonathan Edwards, Jr. in one of many Edwardsian "Schools of the Prophets." His first pastorate was in New Hartford, Connecticut, where he experienced a revival that began in November 1798. Over the next twelve months, one hundred "were hopefully added to the

Lord."[86] The revival also spread from village to village in Litchfield and Hartford counties, an area where churches were led mostly by Edwardsian pastors. Historian David Kling has calculated that thirty Congregational churches in northwest Connecticut admitted 1,699 new converts to membership between 1798 and the end of 1800.[87] Griffin later recalled:

> I saw a continued succession of heavenly sprinklings at New Salem, Farmington, Middlebury, and New Hartford, (all in Connecticut,) until, in 1799, I could stand at my door in New Hartford, Litchfield county, and number fifty or sixty congregations laid down in one field of divine wonders, and as many more in different parts of New England.[88]

By the fall of 1799, Samuel Hopkins was rejoicing in the revival's spread: "A remarkable revival of religion has lately taken place in New England and part of New York State, it is said in more than 100 towns mostly if not wholly under the preachers of Edwardean divinity."[89]

So before the Cane Ridge camp meeting in 1801 and before Timothy Dwight led a revival among his students at Yale in 1802, Edwardsian ministers had already witnessed widespread revival in their Connecticut churches. God had once again visited New England, and he had done so through disciples of Jonathan Edwards. And these revivals were much more like those Edwards had led than the ones Finney would lead in the coming decades.

Church-Centered Revival

These revivals did not occur away from the regular rhythms of life at camp meetings, nor did they flow from the heightened anticipation of a tent meeting, nor were they led by famous traveling evangelists. They occurred in local churches and resulted in converts joining local churches. The revivals were led, almost exclusively, by the preaching and

---

86 Sprague, *Lectures on Revivals of Religion*, 427 (appendix).
87 Kling, *Field of Divine Wonders*, 252.
88 Edward Dorr Griffin, in William Buell Sprague, *Lectures on Revivals of Religion* (Glasgow: William Collins, 1832), 426 (appendix).
89 Samuel Hopkins to John Ryland (draft), 17 October, 1799, Samuel Hopkins Papers, Trask Library.

shepherding of ordained and settled pastors. Other than prayer, these pastors believed that the main means God would use to send revival was "the clear presentation of divine truth." Therefore, the pastors emphasized the importance of preaching the truth. They would hold extra meetings during the week for preaching and discussion of spiritual matters, and exchange pulpits or travel in pastoral teams to serve nearby churches. Rather than minimizing the role of the local church, these pastors sought to heighten the importance of church membership. They abandoned longstanding practices in New England by limiting communion and church membership only to those who gave credible testimony of regeneration.

Theologically Calvinist

The Second Great Awakening has often been viewed as atheological and Arminian. However, the Second Great Awakening is not a uniform story of Arminianization and a declining interest in theology. Jonathan Edwards had "found that no discourses have been more remarkably blessed, than those in which the doctrine of God's absolute sovereignty with regard to the salvation of sinners … have been insisted on."[90] His followers agreed. The revivals they led in Connecticut at the outset of the Second Great Awakening occurred as the clergy preached the doctrines of Calvinism, and their hearers converted not just to Christ, but also to the difficult doctrines of grace taught by their ministers. Regarding the revival in New Hartford, Griffin wrote, "The calvinistic doctrines were the great engines in the hand of the Spirit which assailed and broke the hearts of sinners."[91]

Rather than preaching a positive view of the human will, these pastors aimed to convince their hearers of their total depravity. The human heart, they taught, is opposed to God and thus all unregenerate efforts to gain God's favor were in vain. They constantly pressed the lost to see their sinful inability, and thereby acknowledge their complete

---

90 Edwards, *The Great Awakening*, 4:168.
91 Griffin, Letter on Religious Revival in About Forty Adjacent Parishes.

dependence on God for salvation. As one minister reasoned, "Could they once obtain a clear view of their awful depravity, they would renounce every thought of doing anything to help themselves ... and would lie on their faces in sackcloth and ashes, and think of nothing but to cry, day and night, 'God be merciful to me a sinner.'"[92]

As people were converted they came to believe and cherish these same truths. Griffin offered several examples of converts whose new faith manifested itself in their embrace of Calvinist doctrines like God's sovereignty and election. This convergence of conversion and Calvinism was also common in other towns. Samuel Mills, Sr. reported, "It has been no uncommon thing for the subjects of the work, whose chief distress and anxiety antecedently arose from a sense of their being in the hands of God, unexpectedly to find themselves rejoicing in that very consideration. ... They have ... apparently rejoiced in God's supremacy, and in being at his disposal."[93]

Calm and Ordered

The Second Great Awakening has often been associated with emotional excess and manipulation. Whether it was the intense and sometimes frenzied emotion of frontier camp meetings, or the lawyerly pressure of Finney's anxious seat, conversions were often prompted by and resulted in intense emotional displays. The church-centered, Calvinistic revivals of New England were different on this point as well. In report after report of local church revivals, the pastors described the spiritual intensity of the people manifested in silent and earnest attention to the teaching. Griffin reported a season of revival in his church:

The conferences and public assemblies on the Sabbath or lectures were as still almost as a burying ground. No crying out, no noise or disorder, no symptoms of fanaticism of any kind. The work seemed to be carried on by a still small yet powerful

---

[92] Ibid., 1:375.

[93] *CEM* 1 (July 1800): 29.

and all conquering voice; by the power of divine truth on the mind.[94]

In Somers, the awakening "was not, in a single instance, attended with outcry, or noise."[95] In West Britain, Reverend Jonathan Miller explained, "nothing noisy or tumultuous has been discovered, no outcries or swoonings," but instead, "silent and earnest attention to religious instruction has prevailed."[96]

INFLUENTIAL REVIVALS

So what came out of these Calvinist, church-centered, emotionally restrained revivals? Hundreds of people were converted to Christ and joined local churches. The evidence of an extraordinary work of God is evident on dozens of church rolls during this period. In addition, these same pastors and their churches took the lead in starting America's early missionary organizations. On June 21, 1798, as the revivals were becoming more widespread, these Congregationalist pastors formed the Missionary Society of Connecticut. Their passion to spread the gospel and see revival spread led these same ministers to start the American Board of Commissioners for Foreign Missions, the American Bible Society, Andover Seminary, and the United Foreign Missionary Society. Through these largely forgotten revivals, God fanned a spiritual flame that fueled an unprecedented missionary movement in the 19th century.

REVIVAL VS. REVIVALISM

So if these revivals were so significant, why haven't we heard more about them? The main reason is that by the 1820s, the Second Great Awakening was overtaken by a new theology and new methodology that promised impressive results. As Charles Finney and his new measures began to grow in prominence, Edward Dorr Griffin and others sounded the alarm and sought to push back against what they saw as man-made revivalism. By 1827, Griffin had become the president of Williams College. He urged the graduating class to "show yourselves the friends of revivals." However, he went on to

---

94 Griffin, Letter on Religious Revival in About Forty Adjacent Parishes.
95 *CEM* 1 (July 1800): 19.
96 *CEM* 1 (July 1800): 23.

warn them to "avoid those extravagancies which have often brought a stain upon" revivals in the past, "and prejudiced men against them, and laid fatal stumbling blocks before the blind."[97] One former student recalled that Griffin was "no friend of fanaticism," and that he "opposed all the forms of man-made revivals" and "all methods of getting up revivals by human artifice."[98] When some students, during a campus revival, began to believe that prayer would inevitably lead to conversion, Griffin quickly corrected them.

In 1832, Griffin wrote two letters in which he countered the new measures directly. He criticized the different methods evangelists were using in order to "lead awakened sinners to *commit themselves*." These "maneuvers"—such as calling people to "request public prayers by rising; to come out into the aisle …. to take particular seats, called … 'anxious seats'; [and] to come forward and kneel, in order to be prayed for"—were in danger of leading to "a reliance on other means than truth and prayer, and on other power than that of God." Ministers were calling sinners to form "resolutions" and utter "promises" they were unable to fulfill on their own. Instead of making resolutions, Griffin argued, sinners "must cast themselves instantly on the Holy Ghost."[99]

Though designed to get sinners over their fear of man and awaken others to similar commitment, the new measures tended to lead sinners to a "self-righteous dependence" on their own acts rather than on God. Ministers' reliance on "these newly-invented means of impression" meant that the truths of God's character, human sinfulness, the "provision of the atonement, and terms of acceptance with God" were "very imperfectly brought out, or even studied." Instead, Griffin claimed, evangelists just touched on a "few topics of exhortation," leaving the people "in

---

97 Edward Dorr Griffin, *A Sermon, Preached September 2, 1827, Before the Candidates for the Bachelor's Degree in Williams College* (Williamstown, MA: Ridley Bannister, 1827), 15.

98 Cooke, *Recollections of Rev. E. D. Griffin*, 149.

99 Sprague, *Lectures on Revivals of Religion*, 435-436 (appendix).

ignorance, with a high susceptibility of irregular excitement." This form of revival, he warned, would lead to false conversions and religious sectarianism.

Griffin and his friends like Asahel Nettleton continued to long for revival, and believed their doctrinal system and methods were best fitted to bring it about. Griffin warned that Finney and his followers were teaching the error of "the Arminian self-determining power," and turning salvation into a product of man's methods and will. In this growing civil war, true revival, he feared, would be one of the casualties. He foresaw that the new, man-centered theology would cause those with right theology to draw back from seeking revival. Revivalism, he warned, would cause people to forget revival.

In many ways, Griffin was right. The historical revivals he helped shepherd have largely been forgotten. So too has his vision for biblical revival. Griffin and his fellow pastors certainly did not get everything right. But the revivals they led and their writings can help us more clearly see the dangers of revivalism and more fully believe in possibilities of God-sent revival.

Pentecost: An Earthquake with Ongoing Tremors

By Sinclair Ferguson

In some respects, Pentecost may be viewed as the inaugural revival of the New Testament epoch. Certainly, the description of the conviction of sin experienced, the 'sense of awe' (Acts 2:43) which was evoked, and the detailed model of what church life ought to be (Acts 2:44–47) point in that direction. This is what revival is. We might say that revival is the unstopping of the pent-up energies of the Spirit of God breaking down the dams which have been erected against his convicting and converting ministry in whole communities of individuals, as happened at Pentecost and in the 'awakenings' which have followed.

In these contexts, duplicating the pattern of the Day of Pentecost, the proclamation of Christians appears to possess a special access of 'power' as the Spirit bears witness to Christ along, with, and through the witness of disciples (Jn. 15:26-27; *cf.* Acts 4:33; 6:8; 10:38). This is evident in Philip's mission in Samaria. Paul's letters indicate that he experienced this in a number of strategic centers in the course of his journeys (*e.g.* 1 Cor. 2:4; 1 Thes. 1:5).

The powerful coming of the Spirit by no means solved all problems. The spiritual quickenings which took place always seem to have had mixed consequences and even to have been mixed in character, being open to the destructive influences of spiritual pride and wrong-headedness, as in Corinth. That the same is true in later 'awakenings' in the history of the church should therefore not surprise us.

Jonathan Edwards, the New England theologian of revival, may be guilty of no more than over-emphasis in writing that:

> It may be observed that from the fall of man to our day, the work of redemption in its effect has mainly been carried on by remarkable communications of the Spirit of God. Though there be a more constant influence of God's Spirit always in some degree attending his ordinances, yet the way in which the greatest things have been done towards carrying on the work always has been by remarkable effusions at special seasons of mercy.

Such occasions may well be what is in view in Peter's words in Acts 3:19–20: 'Repent, then, and turn to God, so that your sins may be wiped out, *that times of refreshing may come from the Lord*, and that he may send the Christ...' The order of the clauses here (forgiveness, refreshing, return of Christ) suggests that seasons of renewal and revival are in view.

Thus we find two phenomena in the pattern of Acts. We are given 'case-studies' in the Spirit's activity in personal regeneration and conversion. But it is by the single empowering of the Spirit (first exemplified at Pentecost) that monumental advances take place in the kingdom of Christ. The inaugural outpouring of the Spirit creates ripples throughout the world as the Spirit continues to come in power. Pentecost is the epicenter; but the earthquake gives forth further aftershocks. Those rumbles continue through the ages. Pentecost itself is not repeated; but a theology of the Spirit which did not give rise to prayer for his coming in power would not be a theology of *ruach*!

EDITOR'S NOTE:

This article is excerpted from *The Holy Spirit* by Sinclair Ferguson and is reproduced with permission of the Licensor through PLSclear.

Don't Walk the Aisle, Carry Your Cross

By Ben Lacey

A few weeks back, my wife and I went out on a much-needed date night. Everything was set--we had a babysitter and plans to check out a new and popular Mexican restaurant. The night was going well. We even found parking, a miracle in DC. When we got to the restaurant, I skipped past the long line right up to the receptionist with pride. After all, I had a reservation, and those poor souls didn't.

What happened next was shocking. Our name wasn't on the list. But how could this be? Surely, they'd made an error on their end. I had my reservation, and I could prove it. I opened my phone, eager to prove my good works, only to find out that I had made a reservation for the wrong date. How humiliating. I then proceeded to sincerely plead my case to why they should give us a table--we have three kids with a fourth on the way and date nights are exceedingly rare--but my sincerity wasn't enough.

I imagine that's how many people live their lives today. They think they're right with God when they are not. They are sincere in their assurance. But they are sincerely wrong. Who's to blame for this? Well, ultimately, every man and woman will face the Lord and be held accountable for their own sins. At the same time, at least some blame belongs to a lot of churches and pastors. People like me.

Here's why. A few weeks back, I decided to watch Easter services at gospel-preaching churches all over the country to see how they celebrated resurrection Sunday. What I found was concerning and troublesome. I heard pastors—my brothers in Christ; men who faithfully preach the gospel—say things that undermine the gospel they just preached.

While beckoning people to come to Christ, they led people through the sinner's prayer. A few pastors said something like this, "If you prayed that *prayer sincerely*, the Bible says there is rejoicing in heaven over you, and I want you to walk forward now so we can rejoice with you." At this point, many people flooded the aisles.

Years ago, when I was a youth pastor, I rejoiced over seeing students respond after I gave a similar invitation. Don't get me wrong, I pray and hope that all of those who prayed and walked the aisle were truly born again. But I have my doubts. Why? At least two reasons.

1. THESE INVITATION METHODS ARE BIBLICALLY DEFICIENT.

In Luke 15:7, Jesus doesn't say, "There is rejoicing in heaven over one who prays a prayer, or walks an aisle, or who is spontaneously baptized." No, he says, there is rejoicing in heaven over one sinner who "repents." How does repentance happen? According to Jesus in Luke 15:3–7, it happens when the shepherd leaves the ninety-nine and goes and finds the lost sheep. Repentance happens because the shepherd knows his sheep and won't lose a single one. Jesus is calling his sheep to himself, not through man-made invitation methods, but by pastors faithfully preaching the gospel.

2. THESE INVITATION METHODS CREATE A CRISIS OF ASSURANCE.

Methods like the sinner's prayer, walking an aisle, hyped-up worship music, and spontaneous baptisms are the devil's version of Robin Hood. They give assurance of salvation to those who shouldn't have it, and steal assurance from those who should.

For example, If you say to a group of people, "Do you want to go to heaven and not be eternally punished for your sins in hell?" No one in their right mind will say, "Nah, I'm good!" So you keep going: "Here's how you get to heaven: sincerely pray this prayer, walk the aisle, and get baptized!"

What happens at this moment? Possibly some conversions. Praise God! At the same time, you've probably just assured a bunch of people who haven't counted the cost of following Jesus that they will spend eternity in heaven because of their sincere prayer and immediate obedience to your simple instructions, both of which were emotionally stirred up by a good musical set and the preacher's rhetoric of guilt, fear, and desire. How many non-Christians sit in your pews every Sunday, hardened in their unbelief because they've been given false assurance?

But that type of evangelism is unhelpful even for those whom God really does save because it more or less ensures that they will struggle with assurance. Why? Because you've connected their right standing before God to the sincerity of their prayers and their obedient response to an invitation. Put simply, they're standing on sinking sand. When the emotions fade, when temptations and trials come, when obedience flags and sin seems to rule the day, the poor saints will be gripped with fear and anxiety that they didn't pray the prayer sincerely enough and that God is now suddenly against them.

Pastors, offer people something greater and more secure than their own works. Offer them Christ!

So what's a better alternative to calling people to pray a prayer and to walk an aisle? Here are four things you should do instead:

1. PREACH GOD'S HOLINESS

Sinners will never see themselves clearly until they see God clearly. They need to see that God in his essence is holy and perfect. He needs nothing and no one. He is self-sufficient. He is wise, just, and good in all that he does. There is none like him. And they are enemies of this God. Why? Because they are sinners and have rebelled against him.

2. PREACH MAN'S SINFULNESS

Pastors need to help people feel the weight of their own sin. For the gospel to do its healing work, it first must wound. Before any man can come to Christ, he needs to see that his nature is corrupt. That he not only does wrong but *is* wrong. He must feel and see his miserable state before a Holy God. Commenting on the invitation methods of his own day that were seeking to speed up conversions, Charles Spurgeon once said, "Sometimes we are inclined to think that a very great portion of modern revivalism has been more a curse than a blessing, **because it has led thousands to a kind of peace before they have known their misery**."[100] When a man feels his helplessness before God, he is finally in a place to be helped by God.

3. PREACH CHRIST'S RIGHTEOUSNESS

For years, John Bunyan was grieved and tormented over his sin and saw no way to be reconciled to God. A prayer or responding to an invitation couldn't heal his burdened conscience. What finally freed Bunyan was not his works, but Christ's. Bunyan was converted when he finally realized: "Thy righteousness is in heaven. … I also saw, moreover, that it was not my good frame of heart that made my righteousness better, nor yet my bad frame that made my righteousness worse; **for my righteousness was Jesus Christ himself**, the same yesterday, today, and forever."[101] What makes a sinner right before God is what Christ has accomplished for them on their behalf. They cannot earn this righteousness, but only can receive it by repentance and faith.

---

100 Murray, Iain Hamish. "Apostasy and Calvinism." *Archibald G. Brown: Spurgeon's Successor*, Banner of Truth Trust, Edinburgh, 2011, p. 293.

101 Bunyan, John. "Grace Abounding to the Chief of Sinners." *Grace Abounding to the Chief of Sinners*, The Banner of Truth Trust, Edinburgh, Scotland, 2018, p. 89.

4. CALL THEM TO CARRY THEIR CROSS

If you only preach Christ's righteousness, then you haven't yet preached what the gospel demands. Sinners must be called to respond. How do they respond? Not by walking an aisle, but by carrying their cross. Here is Jesus's invitation to those who would come after him: "If anyone would come after me, let him deny himself and take up his cross and follow me. For whoever would save his life will lose it, but whoever loses his life for my sake and the gospel's will save it" (Mark 8:34–35).

Pastor, you need to preach that same explicit and hard message Jesus did. Here is what your gospel invitation should sound like:

"You want to be made right with God? You want Christ's righteousness? It will cost you everything. You'll have to quit the sins you love. You may lose your job. Your family may hate you. You need to know following Jesus is always right, but rarely is it easy. If you are here to today and you see that losing everything is worth gaining Christ, then this is the place for you. That's what a church is, a people who have counted the cost and are imperfectly denying themselves and carrying their cross. We would love to talk with you after the service about what it means to follow Christ and how to make your faith public and join this church."

This kind of message and invitation doesn't produce quick results. The masses probably won't walk the aisle. It is, however, the means that Christ has entrusted preachers with to call his sheep to himself. So, pastor, model this for your people by denying any desire or method for quick growth and trust that Christ will bring about true and sincere results through the faithful preaching of his gospel.

Can You Reverse Engineer Revival?

By Sean DeMars

The pastry chef takes another bite of thawed dough as she pulls the seventeenth batch of cookies out of the oven, hoping she has *finally* figured out the secret to her grandmother's long lost ooey-gooey chocolate chip cookies recipe.

Meanwhile, scientists from the University of Toronto work backwards, exploring 20,000 genes—one at a time—hoping to deal a death blow to Glioblastoma, the leading cause of cancer deaths in children and young adults.

Previously, the United States and Israel disassembled, studied, and reassembled the Russian MIG aircraft system before returning it to its rightful owner, Cold War–era Soviet Union.

These are three examples of reverse engineering. From software to military technology, physical machinery to biological functions, we live in an age where reverse engineering is possible. The concept is a simple one. In reverse engineering, we:

1. Take something apart
2. See how it works
3. Aim to replicate

Reverse engineering has been used for great good and great harm. Our gut tells us there's nothing we can't tear down, analyze, and recreate. As we grow accustomed to this quasi-superpower, we find ourselves trying to reverse engineer anything and everything, including things that can't be reverse engineered.

WHAT IS REVIVAL?

This article argues that true revival cannot be reverse engineered because it's fundamentally and genuinely a movement of God. John Piper calls revival, "**God doing** among many Christians at the same time or in the same region, usually, what he is doing all the time in individual Christians' lives as people get saved and individually renewed around the world."[102]

Notice two key elements in Piper's definition:

1. God doing something among many that he always does in individual Christians (Psalm 85:6).
2. God is the one doing the saving and renewing.

This definition of revival is useful because it rightly sees God as the main actor. It helps us see that revival cannot be reverse engineered because the will of God cannot be reverse engineered.

We may be able to tear apart a transistor radio, study it, put it back together, and replicate it from what we've learned. We may be able to taste an item from our favorite restaurant and use our refined palate to figure out the ingredients. We may even be able to study the human cell and use the tools of reverse engineering to fight brain cancer.

But we cannot reverse engineer the divine will of God. We cannot tear his will apart, analyze it, and reproduce it (Isa. 14:24, 55:9). We cannot stimulate him, persuade him, or cajole him to move, because he only and always acts in accordance with his eternal purposes (Eph. 1:1, 5, 9, 11).

THE SOVEREIGN SPIRIT

Consider the words of Jesus, as he speaks on the new birth in John

---

[102] https://www.desiringgod.org/interviews/what-is-revival-and-where-do-we-find-it

3: "The wind blows where it wishes, and you hear its sound, but you do not know where it comes from or where it goes. So it is with everyone who is born of the Spirit" (John 3:8).

Jesus is giving us a peek behind the curtain of the new birth. And his point is fairly obvious: God alone makes sinners alive.

Now consider how this applies to revival. Revival is when many receive the new birth in roughly the same time and place. Whether the wind blows on one person, or ten thousand people, or ten million people, it always and only blows where it pleases. Likewise, the Spirit of God does not move according to the will of man, but the will of the Father (John 6:44, 65). We can no more reverse engineer a revival than we can reverse engineer the wind.

This may leave you wondering if revival is completely out of our hands, if there's nothing we can do to see the Spirit of God move powerfully in our midst. It would be useful here to consider the difference between necessary and sufficient conditions.

NECESSARY VS. SUFFICIENT

There are certain conditions *necessary* for revival—in other words, conditions that must be present for revival to happen. Necessary conditions include prayerful dependence on God, a right understanding of the gospel, and the faithful proclamation of Christ as Savior and Lord.

But none of these conditions are *sufficient* for revival. The only sufficient condition for revival is the sovereign movement of the Spirit of God. This is not something we can cause or force. We can plea for the Spirit to move, but we cannot force him to move. We cannot bribe or entice him to action. The Spirit moves according to the eternal, immovable, and unchanging will of God.

This is good news. We are carnal creatures with wimpy visions of the power of God. But when God moves according to his eternally wise purposes, he always does "immeasurably more than all we ask or imagine" (Eph. 3:20).

A TRUSTED WORD FROM AN OLD FRIEND

Reverse engineering allows the hacker to get into your operating system, the tyrannical nation state to uncover technologies that will almost certainly be used for evil, and the corrupt business to circumvent patent and copyright laws. The principles of reverse engineering are dangerous when they're in the wrong hands and then they're applied to spiritual things like evangelism, conversion, and missions. They produce a dramatic excess of sincere but false professions, false assurance, a surge of nominalism, and a watered-down and tarnished witness for the gospel. To put it another way, reverse engineering gives the outward appearance of success in the short-term but hurts evangelism and disciple-making in the long-term.

So, brother pastors, we must labor to excel in establishing the *necessary* conditions for revival, all while remembering that our triune God has predetermined the *sufficient* conditions for revival in eternity past. As Samuel Rutherford said, "Duties belong to us; results belong to God."

How Strong Trellises Promote Strong Vines

By Paul Alexander

A trellis is a framework built to bear the weight of a living vine so the organism can grow freely and bear fruit. If the trellis is too thick or intricate, it inhibits and chokes the vine. If the trellis is too thin or delicate, it collapses under the weight of the fruit. But a simple, sturdy, spacious trellis gives the vine a structure to climb, air to breathe, and room to grow.

The ministry structure of a church is like a trellis—a minimal framework built to facilitate the growth of the organism. The members and their discipling relationships among each other are the branches of the vine that produce the fruit of Christian convictions, new conversions, godly character, and holy conduct (John 15:1–5). The trellis is the institutional structure that holds or harnesses that organic growth so the fruit doesn't fall to the ground and bruise or rot before it ripens. Here's a sampling of some slats in the trellis and how they support the church's vitality.

FOUNDATIONAL DOCUMENTS

The mooring of any church, of course, is the person and work of Jesus as we find him in the Bible. But as soon as we try to describe who Jesus is, we're articulating a *statement of faith*, however informal. To say "we believe in the Bible," we have to be able to show people what we think the Bible actually says—about itself, God, Jesus, the Spirit, mankind, sin, salvation, holiness, the church, the ordinances, and other doctrines. So a statement of faith, ideally signed by all members, anchors us in our shared doctrinal commitments.

Then, a *church covenant*, signed by all prospective members, briefly delineates how we are committing to live together. This part of the trellis stabilizes our expectations of character and conduct among those who will call themselves members.

A *church constitution* explains how we intend to organize the institutional elements of the church and how we intend to get our shared business done. It will answer questions like: How do we make church decisions? How do authority relationships work in the church? Who votes? What do we vote on? How do we take in members, hire pastors, organize staff, and conduct church discipline when necessary? Will officers have term limits?

GOVERNANCE AND OFFICERS

A clear governance structure (such as elder-leadership with congregational governance) helps people see who is responsible for what. For example, in a congregational church, the whole church gathered is the final authority for doctrine (Gal. 1:6–9; 2 Tim. 4:3); dispute (Matt. 18:16–18), discipline (1 Cor. 5), and membership (2 Cor. 2:3). Yet elders are responsible to provide leadership as the main teachers, overseers, and equippers of the congregation (Eph. 4:11–16; 1 Tim. 3:1–7), while deacons are responsible to serve in physical and financial ways that promote, preserve, and repair church unity (Acts 6:1–7; 1 Tim. 3:8).

Beyond this, each member is responsible to pray, love, make disciples, give, attend, and serve, all under the caring oversight of the elders, and in cooperation with the whole congregation. Wisdom and necessity will often require us to have officers like a treasurer to handle the church's offerings with integrity, or a clerk to record conversations and decisions from members' meetings.

MEMBERSHIP AND MEETINGS

One of the most important parts of the trellis is local church membership. Clarifying the duties and privileges of membership enables people to see how the church understands the biblical means, metrics, and milestones for Christian maturity.

The weekly meetings of the church (e.g., adult education, Sunday morning worship, Sunday evening prayer, a midweek study) provide programmatic opportunities to gather for feeding on God's Word preached, read, sung, and prayed, and for seeing the gospel illustrated in baptism and the Lord's Supper. Periodic business/members' meetings—for us, they're quarterly—give the congregation regular access to the trellis and input on where the next sections might be built. New members' classes teach people where on the trellis they can get engrafted into the visible vine.

STAFF AND SALARIES

Some of our brothers will become so fruitful in their teaching and discipling that we'll want to set them aside for that work by paying them as staff pastors; in other words, their part of the trellis needs to be stronger to support more fruit. Others we'll want to employ more specifically as associate pastors or train as pastoral assistants and interns. Still other members may show themselves skilled enough to be paid as secretaries or ministry directors.

Our staff are the living load-bearers of the ministry who support the vine's growth and vitality, so it's worth paying them well for their work so they can devote themselves to it without distraction (1 Tim. 5:17–18).

BUILDINGS AND BUDGETS

Thankfully, we don't need to own a church building to be an effective church. But a church building does help provide a reliable gathering space and a visibly rooted presence in our community. In our own church's experience, procuring a facility encouraged some distant members to move into neighborhoods closer to the building.

Church-owned residential housing, while again not a must, can provide longer-term hospitality otherwise unavailable to missionaries, interns, entry-level staff, or in some locales, pastors themselves. Budgets, while nowhere commanded in Scripture, help us plan our ministry expenses wisely while taking calculated risks as we trust God's provision.

PROGRAMS

Ministry programs can be useful if they're providing structure for what we find onerous to do naturally. Age and affinity-based relationships (singles, young-marrieds, golden girls, athletics, sowing) happen instinctively. Programs are usually best saved to prod us into ministries we find less natural or more demanding of congregational energy, whether that's small group accountabilities, systematic doctrinal instruction, children's ministries, or the like.

A vine will likely languish just lying on the ground, and its fruit can die on the vine. A rickety lattice will either blow over in the wind, or sag and splinter under the weight of the fruit. But if you drape your vine over a simple trellis with structural integrity, then its fruit is far more likely to mature without bruising.

Pray for Revival—in the Other Guy's Church

By Andy Johnson

What if you spent years faithfully and earnestly praying for revival to come to your community, and then one day, seemingly out of the blue, God dramatically answered your prayers?

All across your city, every day people begin crowding into the church to hear the gospel from God's Word. On the streets, in their workplaces, in classrooms and homes all over town, previously timid church members are faithfully declaring the gospel and fruit is coming fast. Lives are transformed, marriages are saved, and most of all, one after another God's enemies are laying down the weapons of their rebellion and are taking refuge in his glorious and merciful Son.

What if all this happened in your own town, right in front of your eyes, in that other guy's church, just a few blocks down the street from yours?

I suspect we all know what we ought to say in response, but the words of praise and joy are likely to get caught in the backs of our throats.

This has happened before. In 1839 Robert Murray M'Cheyne learned that a great revival had broken out in his church under a guest preacher while he was away on a months-long mission trip. When the Spirit of God seems to bless the ministry of others rather than our own, some pretty important things about the real nature of our loves become glaringly visible.

"DIOTREPHES, WHO LOVES TO BE FIRST"

Of course, this battle between envy and rejoicing is nothing new. The Apostle John writes about the issue in his third letter (3 John). There, in verses five to eleven, he introduces us to two men: Gaius and Diotrephes.

Gaius loves to welcome and support faithful missionaries sent out from other churches because he loves Jesus (vv. 5-8).

Diotrephes, well…not so much. Diotrephes refuses to welcome these workers from other churches for one simple reason: John tells us plainly that Diotrephes "loves to be first" (v. 9). He has no desire to see gospel work done unless he does it. He will rejoice in no fruit unless it's his fruit. He will tolerate no competition. Diotrephes' actions and attitudes are, John's bluntly says, simply "evil" (v. 11).

Evil—that's a strong word. And frankly what frightens me most about Diotrephes is that we're not told of any lack of doctrinal orthodoxy to justify that label. There is no mention of heresy or inadequate views of Christ. For all we know, Diotrephes' theology looked just right on paper. But his competitive spirit exposed his supposed love for the gospel as merely love for his own group, his own ministry—ultimately love for himself. Just like any other pagan.

THE NOT-SO-SUBTLE POINT

So here comes the not-so-subtle point of this article: Do not be like Diotrephes! Instead, imitate what is good, meaning the gospel-exalting, non-competitive spirit of Gaius.

But why is this such a big deal? Because not only your heart but the very worth of the gospel in the eyes of the world is at stake.

Listen, you can talk all day about how you praise God for the blessings of gospel prosperity in your church—and you should, to some extent. And yet there will always be a lingering scent of self-interest; it's your church, after all.

But what if you genuinely praise God for the gospel prosperity in some other church, whether in another country or even (gulp) right across town? What if you demonstrate the same delight to see Jesus' work held up and delighted in as a result of someone else's ministry? If you do, that shows that you love Jesus and his gospel and his glory—not just your group, your club, your ministry, your church.

That's why it's so important that we cultivate an attitude like Gaius' in our hearts and in our church members' hearts. Our love for Jesus and for his glory may never shine brighter than when we rejoice in the progress of the gospel even when there isn't the slightest chance of us getting any of the credit.

HOW TO CULTIVATE THE SPIRIT OF GAIUS

How can you cultivate this kind of spirit in your church and in your own heart? Here are a few ways.

1. Pray and Read

First, pray and read. Start by reflecting on passages like 3 John that show the unique glory of what we might call a "disinterested delight" in the prosperity of the gospel. And pray that God would grow in you a heart that loves to encourage gospel progress, wherever it happens and whoever it happens through. Why? Because you love to see Jesus glorified.

2. Model and Teach

Second, model and teach. Show your church what this looks like by regularly praying for other faithful churches, by name, in public, from your pulpit, on Sunday morning. Praise God openly for the prosperity he may be giving to other churches that preach the same gospel, even right there in your own town. And pray for Christians and gospel work in other places around the world, too. Teach your people by this that the kingdom of God is much, much bigger than your local church.

3. Support and Celebrate

Third, support and celebrate. And, like faithful Gaius, go all the way and take money you could really use for your own church and give it away. Give it to bless other churches and to support faithful workers who have been sent out for the sake of the name (3 John 7). Again, when your church sends its money to bless and support external gospel work it's like a megaphone announcing, "We love Jesus and his glory, not just our own group and our ministry."

Certainly you have to keep some money to responsibly care for your own congregation. I understand that. But do you really need all the money God gives you? Really? Might it not be wonderfully liberating and gospel-clarifying to write a check that declares your church is free, through the grace of God, from the bondage of exclusive self-interest? True churches are not in competition with each other for dollars, or members, or glory. After all, all the money, all the people, and all the glory belong to God.

MAY WE PRAISE GOD FOR OTHER CHURCHES' SUCCESS—AND MEAN IT

God has a big plan for his whole world, and God will accomplish his work in the world. He will save his children, and secure them in the faith, and grow them in holiness.

Sometimes he may do that through us. Sometimes he may do it through the church down the street. May we grow in our love for the glory of Christ so that either way we can say "Praise God," and really mean it.

How Movements Can Undermine Churches and Hurt Their Own Cause

By Jonathan Leeman

Part of my PhD work involved exploring the "new institutionalism" that began surfacing in political science departments in the 1980s.

Prior to the eighties, the field of political science was fairly anti-institutional. Instead, it was beholden to behaviorism and behaviorism's emphasis on the motivations of individual actors. Institutions were just big clunky machines we were forced to drive to get where we want. Yet little by little these departments began to realize that institutions are much more dynamic. Actors and institutions implicate and shape one another. Institutions might slow us down, but they also grow and fashion us—our identity and sense of purpose.

The same is true more broadly. People instinctively grimace at the thought of "institutions" because they constrain us. They keep us from moving and growing in ways that feel natural. But look a little closer. Those constraints also facilitate, channel, and stimulate growth. A trimmed rose bush grows. Lines on the road help us reach our destination. Games are most enjoyable when people keep the rules. Mastering a language gives us power. In short, institutions allow for "bounded innovation," as one political scientist put it. They curtail the excessive, unwieldy growth that ultimately harms the cause, while creating exponential potential previously unimagined.

Charles Spurgeon, with his useful foresight and instinctive genius, anticipated what took political scientists another century to figure out as he meditated on the relationship of revivals and church membership in his sermon "The Great Revival":

> I must say, once more, that if God should send us a great revival of religion, it will be our duty not to relax the bonds of discipline. Some churches, when they increase very largely, are apt to take people into their number by wholesale, without due and proper examination. We ought to be just as strict in the paroxysms of a revival as in the cooler times of a gradual increase, and if the Lord sends his Spirit like a hurricane, it is ours to deal with skill with the sails lest the hurricane should wreck us by driving us upon some fell rock that may do us serious injury. Take care, ye that are officers in the church, when ye see the people stirred up, that ye exercise still a holy caution, lest the church become lowered in its standard of piety by the admission of persons not truly saved.

Spurgeon's wisdom bears worth repeating in our own day. The good desire for a God-given revival quickly morphs into man-manufactured revivalism as Christians get more excited about the ideas of movements than they do about the clunky old local church. One generation of pastors and missionaries will announce a massive number of conversions with fireworks, while a second generation will show up ten years later, look around, and ask, "Where did all those new converts go?" like peaking into an empty convention hall with nothing but folding chairs and trash left behind.

THE TEMPTATION OF REVIVALISM

Yet the temptation of revivalism is understandable. So often the work of the local church feels slow, unimpressive, even unproductive. Week after week another sermon, the same songs, folks shuffling in and shuffling out. Meanwhile, evangelistic encounters feel like banging one's head on the wall. No one's interested in our good news. No one's buying. Baptisms happen, but not nearly as quickly as we trust our sovereign God is capable of giving.

Then people talk of a movement, and our ears perk up. Who of us, from the earliest days of our faith, has not wanted to witness a revival or get swept up in a movement? To watch as a river of people rush toward Jesus, having just discovered his goodness and grace. The call to join the movement may involve self-sacrifice, but it holds up a shared vision and the hope of explosive growth, which feels compelling after years of schlepping and knocking on closed doors.

LOOSENING THE CONSTRAINTS OF A CHURCH

To this end, the leaders of movements loosen the tight, institutional strictures of a local church, like unbuckling a belt. Now we can really run! Think of D. L. Moody's decision to decline ordination since, as one friend said to him, being a "preaching layman" would be an "advantage." Employing lay preachers would allow for quicker reduplication, never mind the old habit of theological training (Murray, *Revival and Revivalism*, 360). Or think of Billy Graham, calling people to come forward by the thousands, yet sending them to any number of churches with little regard for denominational differences. Or think of how mission agencies today sometimes designate two or three new converts who regularly meet together as a "church" in their reporting, or how they loosen the requirements for leadership or membership.

In his article "Six Marks of Revivalism," historian Andrew Ballitsch lists "inadequate ecclesiology" as one of the marks. He observes that revivalism, by its very nature, "looks beyond the ordinary means of grace" and "undervalue[s] the power and centrality of ordinary local church ministry." In the nineteenth-century version, he explains open-air preaching and tent meetings even replaced the local church. Not surprisingly, revivalism's lack of emphasis on the local church was coupled with an "ambivalence toward denominational forms." This in turn "set the stage for undenominational evangelists like D. L. Moody and Ira Sankey" on the one hand, while on the other hand resulted in the "promulgation of numerous denominations and radical sects that claimed to be the harbingers of true religion."

WHAT CONSTRAINTS ARE NECESSARY?

The point here is not to condemn all movements. When God hears the prayers of his people and decides to give an unusual quantity of conversions and gospel obedience, we should rejoice. Yet movements need all the biblically assigned constraints of local churches. And it's all those constraints—a church's governance, membership, discipline practices, and the ordinary means of grace generally—that in turn create genuine movements, not man-manufactured, fake-O ones. Like the political scientists discovered, movements and churches implicate and shape one another, strengthening each other.

What constraints are necessary? The very things that make a church a church in the Bible. A church is:

- a group of born-again, baptized Christians
- who gather
- weekly on the Lord's Day
- in a regular, predictable location
- to preach the Bible
- and mutually affirm one another's profession and discipleship in the Supper
- while baptizing still others
- under the leadership of elders.

Each of these constraints is biblical and necessary for preserving the dynamism of a movement, whether the movement is massive or tiny. Remove any one, and corruptions or nominalism will follow. A weak understanding of conversion or being born-again will allow a church to fill up with people who might offer sincere but false professions. A group that doesn't regularly gather cannot spur one another on to love and good deeds as the Day approaches. A group that doesn't gather in one place is hard for outsiders to find. A church whose preaching is biblically thin will only produce thin Christians. And so forth.

With biblical strictures loosened or even forgotten, movements begin to unravel. Apart from the support of a trellis, the grape vine bends back on its own weight or grows in directions it shouldn't. Or it just dies.

From their earliest history, therefore, Baptists have taken great care in defining a church, because our churches should be the origin and locus of any disciple-making movements that occur. The 1644 London Baptist Confession defined a church as a "company of visible saints called and separated from the world, by the Word and the Spirit of God, to the visible profession of the faith of the Gospel, being baptized into the faith, and joined to the Lord, and each other, by mutual agreement, in the practical enjoyment of the ordinances, commanded by Christ their head and King." For the saints to be "visible," they must meet all together and regularly in one place. For them to be a "company" of saints, there must be the "mutual agreement" over one another's professions, as revealed in the ordinances. A church is not just three new converts regularly meeting. And has the movement of Baptist churches grown since 1644? Beyond measure.

NEEDED: CHURCH-DRIVEN MINISTRY

In short, what pastors, missionaries, and campus leaders need is a vision for church-driven ministry, not movement-driven ministry. This requires paying careful attention to our ecclesiology, even if building a healthy church is slow, sometimes cumbersome work. This is how we build for the long-run, not for the sprint. Then let the movements swell as God gives them. Quite simply, the Bible places the local church and its devices into our hands, while God keeps the starting of movements in his own hands.

"Take care," says Spurgeon to pastors, "when ye see the people stirred up, that ye exercise still a holy caution, lest the church become lowered in its standard of piety by the admission of persons not truly saved." And "We ought to be just as strict in the paroxysms of a revival as in the cooler times of a gradual increase."

Why Revivalism Causes Pastors to Burn Out and Job-Hop

By Phil A. Newton

Revivalism shaped my early Christian faith. Preaching went light on the Word and heavy on coaxing spiritual decisions. Many congregations measured a pastor's effectiveness by the number of public responses he received at the close of the service; no one ever talked about faithfulness in doctrinal exposition. Scripture was often taken out of context, and no one seemed to notice or care. *Ho-hum subjects* such as the ordinary means of grace, personal discipline, and perseverance resulting in Christ formed in believers by Word and Spirit rarely came on the radar of worship gatherings.

In short, revivalism was alive and well in twentieth-century pastoral ministry. Just as in the previous century, it burned over local communities and cultivated an obsession with numbers and decisions. Meanwhile, cynicism and apathy toward biblical Christianity increased, while healthy pastors and churches decreased.

I preached my first sermon at the ripe age of sixteen. I was affected by what I heard and observed as normal Christian practice in my region. My lack of biblical moorings soon sapped my spiritual life. Revivalism was a poor tutor for this aspiring pastor. I desperately needed to heed this instruction from Francis Grimké: "From beginning to end, all effective work is due to the presence and power of the Spirit in the preacher and in the people to whom he speaks. ... There is no other guarantee of success. There is no other power that can bring results ... and bring men to repentance and faith."[103]

Understanding dependence on the Word and Spirit would have reoriented my entire approach to and practice of pastoral ministry. But instead, I struggled to make sense of the man-centered revivalism I'd been taught.

EVIDENCE OF TRUE SPIRITUAL WORK

Revivalism seeks to reproduce what only God can accomplish. The 18th century's Great Awakening, under the human instrumentation of Jonathan Edwards, George Whitefield, and others, witnessed distinct evidence of divine work. Edwards identified this evidence as:

- Esteem for the person and work of Jesus, in dependence on his redemptive work.
- Overcoming the spirit of the world through the work of the Spirit.
- A high regard for and reliance on Holy Scripture.
- Hearts inclined to the truth of Scripture.
- By the new life in Christ, loving God and man.[104]

The Second Great Awakening, which began toward the close of the 18th century, experienced something similar. There seemed to be a revival at Yale under Edwards' grandson Timothy Dwight's leadership. But as evidence of God's sovereign work of revival waned, man-centered techniques stepped in to fill the void. This process was largely led by Charles G. Finney.

---

103 Francis James Grimké, *Meditations on Preaching* (Madison, MS: Log College Press, 2018), 2.

104 Jonathan Edwards, *Jonathan Edwards on Revival* (Edinburgh: The Banner of Truth Trust, 1984, from the 1741 edition of *Distinguishing Marks of a Work of the Spirit of God*), 109–120.

Still in my teens, I remember reading a slim biography of Finney. The author engaged in hero adulation, ignoring Finney's erroneous soteriology, man-centered preaching, and negative long-term effects on the church. As I read about Finney calling people to make decisions, I fell into the same trap. Finneyism became my calling.

Finney's plan to win converts involved contracted meetings that lasted anywhere from a week to several weeks. He relied on invitation methods to manipulate decisions and assumed professions of faith without evidence of regeneration. This led to confusion about true conversion. Steeped in these practices, my spiritual life sagged and I needed renewal. Instead of learning to grow in Christ through the ordinary means of grace, I joined my friends in flocking anywhere revivalism was happening. I didn't know anything else.

THE HOOK OF REVIVALISM

I attended countless so-called *revivals* (contracted meetings) in my first half-dozen years as a Christian. Crowded altars, as they were termed, followed emotionally driven sermons. Professing Christians *rededicated* their lives over and over. The new birth seemed to live in the shadows of revivalism, not at the forefront. Later, it became shockingly clear to me: whenever we move away from a dependence on the Word of God and the Spirit of God for Christian ministry, we may see results, but they won't be God-birthed results.

Those same people made decisions over and over because the gospel was not clearly proclaimed; no one wanted to be patient for the Spirit's work. These repeated public decisions led to swelling church rolls. I knew the gospel was supposed to produce perseverance, but I was surrounded by impatience. In that era, Gardiner Spring observed, "There is one grace you cannot counterfeit … the grace of *perseverance*."[105] So little was made of perseverance because

---

105 Iain H. Murray, *Revival & Revivalism: The Making and Marring of American Evangelicalism 1750–1858* (Edinburgh: The Banner of Truth Trust, 1994), xv, citing Gardiner Spring, *Personal Reminiscences of the Life and Times of Gardiner Spring* (New York, 1866), vol. 1, 217–18.

it contradicted what pastors attempted to do with revivalism practices.

Why did pastors who claimed to believe the Bible persist with unbiblical methods in preaching? Why did they ignore biblical ecclesiology? It's hard to say. But I can't help but wonder if all the decisions and the large crowds simply appealed to their pride and satisfied their vanity. Depending on the Word and waiting on the Spirit isn't flashy.

REVIVALISM'S PASTORAL DOWNSIDE

To sustain its adherents, revivalism demands an increasing intensity. More meetings, more emotional appeals, more extended "invitations," and more high-profile personalities keep people engaged.

Unregenerate people, convinced they are backslidden Christians, respond to appeals to rededicate their lives at the close of a meeting. And they are freshly devoted—at least for a few weeks. But over time, without the regenerating work of the Spirit, they slip into nominal Christianity. Meanwhile, the pastor, whose *gifts* and *pulpit skills* helped to coax the decisions, may unknowingly slide into pride over his power to make things happen. As he continues to see many make decisions at his appeal, pride builds. In place of a humble dependence upon the Holy Spirit and gospel proclamation, he begins to lean on his abilities.

Over time, these practices shape a pastor's habits. They become ingrained into his psyche. He may feel guilt, not over neglecting the Word and Spirit, but for his failure to draw a crowd and provoke enough decisions. He feels pressure from ministry colleagues to increase productivity through techniques used by other high-profile revivalist preachers. But the more responses he sees, the more he slides deeper into self-dependence. The more he falls away from reflecting the humble ministry of Jesus in John 13.

Ultimately, many pastors who depend on revivalist practices burn out because they've never learned to depend not on themselves but on the Word and Spirit. They burn out because they're aiming at evident fruitfulness, not unremarkable faithfulness. Revivalist pastors burn out or job-hop. After all, once his church stops responding to his methods, he moves to another pulpit where he will yet again fail to patiently teach God's Word.

Perhaps these reflections seem exaggerated. But consider: if a pastor fails to minister in dependence upon the Word and Spirit, then what sustains him? Whatever it is, it will fail to endure. Revivalism saps the pastor's life because it offers only a veneer of Christianity. Only dependence upon the gospel of Christ and power of the Spirit will build churches on the power of God rather than the wisdom of man (1 Cor. 2:1–5).

The Revival We Need and the Unregenerate Church Members We Have

By Jim Elliff

In the early 1700s, between 75 and 80 percent of American people attended church meetings regularly. Yet huge numbers among them were unconverted. It was among these people that Awakening doctrines had their greatest effects. In other words, wherever people gathered, within or outside the colonial church buildings, the principle leaders were addressing church members who needed Christ.

What truth, among the many emphasized, had the greatest influence on unconverted church members in The Great Awakening? And who are the unconverted church members in our context who may also need this truth?

*****

THE GREAT AWAKENING EMPHASIS ON REGENERATION

When George Whitefield was asked why he so often preached, "Ye must be born again," he replied, "Because ye must be born again!"

Regeneration, or the new birth, was the prevalent issue of the Great Awakening of the 1740s. As Joseph Tracey said:

> This doctrine of the "new birth," as an ascertainable change, was not generally prevalent in any communion when the revival commenced; it was urged as of fundamental importance, by the leading promoters of the revival; it took strong hold of those whom the revival affected; it naturally led to such questions as the revival brought up and caused to be discussed; its perversions naturally grew into, or associated with, such errors as the revival promoted; it was adapted to provoke such opposition, and in such quarters, as the revival provoked; and its caricatures would furnish such pictures of the revival, as oppressors drew. This was evidently the right key; for it fitted all the wards of the complicated lock.[106]

This doctrine has repeatedly been at the heart of awakenings.

By "regeneration," we mean the giving of life to dead souls as a sovereign work of the Holy Spirit. Berkhof says it is "that act of God by which the principle of the new life is implanted in man, and the governing disposition of the soul is made holy ... and the first holy exercise of this new disposition is secured."[107] The Lord lived and died for his own, and as King, gifts our dead souls with new life resulting in sight, belief, repentance, and holiness.

J.C. Ryle said in so many words that the awakening preachers of that time believed in an indivisible union between authentic faith and holiness. He writes, "They never allowed for a moment that any church membership or religious profession was the least proof of a man being a Christian if he lived an ungodly life."[108]

The attention to this truth, fed by their earlier Puritan theology, brought great conviction

---

106 Joseph Tracey, *The Great Awakening* (Edinburgh: Banner of Truth, reprint 1976), ix.

107 Louis Berkhof, *Systematic Theology* (Grand Rapids: Eerdmans, 1939, 1988), 469.

108 J. C. Ryle, *Christian Leaders of the 18th Century* (Edinburgh: Banner of Truth, reprint 1978), 28.

and massive numbers of conversions when preached and taught with the unction of the Spirit in times of revival. Where it did not bring conviction, it brought anger. Whitefield, who himself was written against in over 240 tracts of various types,[109] said that when you heard middle colonies' preacher Gilbert Tennent (and his brothers) you were either converted or enraged. According to Gillies' quoting of Prince in *Historical Collections of Accounts of Revival*, Tennent is said to have preached in this way:

Such were the convictions wrought in many hundreds in this town by Mr. Tennent's searching ministry; and such was the case of those many scores of several other congregations as well as mine, who came to me and others for direction under them. And indeed, by all their converse I found, it was not so much the terror as the searching nature of his ministry that was the principal means of their conviction. It was not merely, nor so much, his laying open the terrors of the law and wrath of God, or damnation of hell (for this they could pretty well bear, as long as they hoped these belonged not to them, or they could easily avoid them), as his laying open their many vain and secret shifts and refuges, counterfeit resemblance's of grace, delusive and damning hopes, their utter impotence, and impending danger of destruction; whereby they found all their hopes and refuges of lies to fail them, and themselves exposed to eternal ruin, unable to help themselves, and in a lost condition. This searching preaching was both the suitable and principal means of their conviction.[110]

Hundreds came in those days after Gilbert Tennent preached on his early ministry tour, more than most of the local pastors had seen in the entirety of their ministries.

---

109 Bob Roberts, International Awakening Ministries, from an unpublished paper.

110 John Gillies, *Historical Collections of Accounts of Revival*, as quoted from Prince (Edinburgh: Banner of Truth, reprint 1981), xii.

THE UNREGENERATE CHURCH MEMBERS IN NEED OF AWAKENING

As in the period prior to the Great Awakening, unregenerate church members abound in our day. Who are the unregenerate church members in need of awakening? We must begin answering the above question by saying that those church members who profess to know Christ yet do not come to the assembly at all, or who come only occasionally, are on the main unregenerate. If you believe I am too acute by categorizing most non-attending members as unregenerate and think that coming to church is not specifically given in Scripture as a mark of the Christian, consider what failure to attend indicates. It tells us that the professed believer does not love the brethren, need the teaching of the Bible, relish the corporate worship of God, or acknowledge submission to God-ordained leadership. In general, the one who does not come says that the environment of believers is not his preferred environment. Perhaps because he is more satisfied with the world.

To illustrate our problem, in 2018, one beloved historic Southern Baptist Church whose name most Baptists would recognize claimed 30,000 members and an average of 6,801 attending. It was noted as the top church in baptisms among the SBC for 2018) at 682 persons.

If there are approximately 300 non-member children and 100 guests (a conservative guess) attending each week, the number would be something like 6,401 actual members attending on average weekly. That means approximately 21.3 percent of the church attends every week. Even if my numbers are off by a lot, the point remains the same. Churches that are smaller have less of a disparity in the SBC, usually somewhere between 35 and 40 percent attend on a given Sunday in those. This is alarming. And the problem exists in most denominations.

One of the distressing tangents to this problem is that many who are promoting revival in our day, and are the most outspoken, are the very ones most responsible for this disparity between the actually converted and the numbers on the rolls. If revival will come, I fully suspect that many leaders whose ministries are yielding the greatest numbers of unregenerate professors of faith will need to repent of this careless, blatant disregard for souls.

Often there are the finest of intentions. But that doesn't excuse the startling lack of perception of the problem. Next month they will have yet another campaign to bring people in, 70 percent of which (or more) will eventually show the signs of being unconverted.

Who are the unregenerate church members who need to be awakened? They are not only those who do not come, but those who do not know Christ (i.e. enjoy intimacy with him) even if they do attend, because knowing Christ is the heart of eternal life (Jn. 17:3; Heb. 8:11). This was also the case in the colonial period when so many attended as a matter of principle and habit.

The unregenerate are also those who have no fruit of holiness or consistently bear bad fruit. (Mt. 7:21–23; Heb. 12:14; 1 Cor. 6:9-11). They are those who are not repentant (Acts 17:30; Jn. 2:23-25) and those who do not have persevering faith (Lk. 8:13; 1 Pet. 1:3-9). I have written elsewhere of these issues and will not belabor them now. But I will note this: our churches are filled with people who do not have the evidences of spiritual life, yet sincerely believe they are right with God.

An Appeal

My intent in this short article is to alert you in an introductory way how the doctrine of regeneration was used in arguably the most important and powerful of the historical awakenings, and to remind you that there are similarly many deceived church members all around us who need to be confronted with the same truth.

Pastor, you need to labor hard to know this doctrine well. Prepare yourself and those you lead by serious study on the subject. Like a physician prepares by deep consideration of the anatomy, give yourself to intense preparation related to this doctrine. Search for yourself through Scripture to see clearly the way the biblical characters and writers taught how life from God enters the dead soul and radically transforms the person. Though it has not been the purpose of this short article to explore the array of older and newer theological expressions of the doctrine, they are readily available. Make yourself a student of this powerful truth. Also, read the history of the First Great Awakening for yourself to see how God has used this doctrine.

By helping confused and often deceived church members explore whether or not they have been made alive, you will find this doctrine to be the most helpful. Leaders who neglect this doctrine will perpetuate the increase of unregenerate church members in our churches.

Having been in many churches as an itinerant Bible teacher, I have consistently found that the churches that seem to be the strongest often have many members who have worked through earlier deceptions about their conversion to arrive at a solid assurance with God. The probing was occasioned by learning that spiritual life in the individual produces noticeable change. The exploration into whether or not they actually have spiritual life altered everything.

This has been my experience as a pastor as well. How often I have heard the best of members say that when they learned of what the life of God in the soul of the believer exhibits, they discovered that they had never been given that life. Or, conversely, they discovered that they do have such life in them, thus giving them new assurance and boldness.

EDITOR'S NOTE

This article is adapted and revised from "Revival and the Unregenerate Church Member," by Jim Elliff, originally published in *Reformation and Revival Journal*.

Revivalism on the Mission Field

By Scott Logsdon

I have many missionary friends who are faithful ministers of the gospel. Each morning, they rise to spend time in devoted study of the Bible and prayer and then spend the rest of the day urging their national friends to consider Christ. They creatively turn conversations to the gospel. They patiently consider each person's needs and life situation. They faithfully pray for their friends and others in their cities to be raised from death to life.

These missionary friends hear stories of missionaries in other places who have seen many people rapidly come to Christ. They know that such events are *possible*. After all, the book of Acts tells of 3,000 coming into God's kingdom in a day, and another 2,000 within a short period. Church history recounts awakenings and revivals where many souls were saved under the preaching of God's Word. These accounts burn in my friends' hearts: they would love to see such revival among the people they serve.

But revival—"a sovereign and large giving of the Spirit of God, resulting in the addition of many to the kingdom of God"—shouldn't be confused with revivalism.

WHAT IS REVIVALISM?

Revivalism is the practice of using methods to pursue or even cause a "revival." It's a relatively new phenomenon that assumes a particular view of conversion. Revivalistic practices were developed during the Second Great Awakening (1800–1825). In these twenty-five years, an extraordinary harvest of men and women responded to the gospel and were incorporated into the church. Debate ensued. Did revivalistic practices cause the harvest, or did they cause harm to the church while God gave growth?

At its heart, the issue that separates revival and revivalism is whether these large in-gatherings of new Christians are "normal" or "extraordinary" or not. Veteran pastors and preachers of the First Great Awakening were convinced that the response of the crowds during this period was extraordinary. They had good reason to think so. They knew they had done nothing different than what they had always done: they continued to devote themselves to prayer, they faithfully proclaimed the Scriptures, they urged non-Christians to repent and believe in Christ, and they served and shepherded church members to faithful obedience.

Then one day, the results of their work changed—using words like "sudden" and "unexpected," these men described large numbers of people responding with repentance and faith to their teaching. Other pastors like Whitefield preached another twenty years after the end of the revival he witnessed. During that time, he saw a sudden *decrease* of response to the same preaching. Put simply, a revival happens when pastors do nothing different or more than the faithful, normal means described in the Bible—and yet, the Lord of the Harvest causes an extraordinary increase.

A few decades later, a new generation of pastors would come who tried to build on the foundations for which others labored (John 4:38). These young pastors gathered in the harvest of others' work and began to feel they had discovered the power to sway crowds to become Christians. Revivalist preachers made bold promises: use their methods and conversions can be guaranteed. If Christians will just get to work, then they can convert the world and bring the millennium within a few years. Who *wouldn't* want this to take place?

Whether or not God moved invisibly and spiritually in the hearts of listeners was uncertain. What was certain was that many people responded in a way that could be seen. Over time, this outward activity came to be understood as proof that God was at work and the listeners had been converted. By the end of the nineteenth century, the assumptions of the younger revivalist pastors had become the status quo among American evangelical Christians. Revivalist practices like "coming forward" and altar calls persisted through the popularity of later evangelical preachers, from D. L. Moody to Billy Graham.

REVIVALISM AND MISSIONS

Revivalism's bold promises remain alluring to missionaries. I recall reading one missionary's field report to the home staff. It revealed his strong belief in the power of revivalist practices. Before those practices were used in his area of the world, he reported no conversions. But afterward? Conversions came quickly and persistently. This was more than simply a report. It also seemed to me a subtle promise: if you want to see conversions, then you should practice these methods too.

But let the minister beware. Revivalist practices accompany particular theological and doctrinal assumptions about the nature of conversion, the relationship between proclamation and conversion, and the nature of humans.

CONVERSION

Conversion occurs when God raises someone from death to life (Eph 2:4–9). This entails receiving a new nature, a new heart, and a new disposition from God, all of which allow a person to understand what he or she could not before. Without a new nature, we are unable to believe (John 3:3, 10:26; Acts 16:14). This change of nature cannot be caused or coerced, no sooner than we can force a leopard to change its spots. Instead, the Bible describes conversion as "rebirth" "by the Spirit"; it happens when and where he wishes (John 3:8).

Therefore, missionaries should exercise a little bit of caution before quickly assuring a new professor that they have been born again. The point here is not to wait for evidence of maturity. It's to wait just long enough to see that an initial profession is more than just a momentary flash in the pan. If conversion comes from the Lord, what's true today will be true in a week or in a month. If the conversion is just a passing emotion, it's more likely to dissipate like the mist.

For instance, I once spent two hours with a Muslim friend summarizing the big story of the Bible. I showed him how a dozen Old Testament stories all worked together to anticipate the coming of Christ before I urged him to repent and place his faith in Jesus. He responded, "I want to follow Jesus as Lord for as long as I live!" A revivalist missionary would have then assured my friend that he had been converted and immediately baptized him. Kind of like they always say: "Once decided, always saved."

I simply said what I knew to be true: "I hope so. Let's see how you do over time!" Within one month, he sadly recanted his statement.

Another Muslim man asked a national Christian evangelist friend of mine with revivalistic tendencies what he must do to convert to Christianity. My friend responded, "Just like there's a Muslim confession of faith, there's a Christian confession of faith." Instead of teaching him the depths of his sin, he taught him to confess Christ like Muslims confess Muhammad. Then he led him in a brief sinner's prayer. And that was that! Sadly, this man also returned to Islam.

On another occasion, a Muslim friend studied the Bible with us faithfully for weeks. He loved joining us and reading Scripture. They were words of life to him. One morning as we began our study, he asked whether he could start our time by reading a prayer. He wasn't sure that reading prayers was allowed, but this particular prayer articulated well what he wanted to say. Somewhere, in his studies, he came across a printed sinner's prayer and began to pray aloud. At the close of his prayer, we did not declare him converted. This man, somewhere along the way, had been converted as far as we can tell. He's still following Jesus today.

Conversion is hard. Harder than a camel going through an eye of a needle. Conversion requires power over men's souls, and only God holds that power. Physical and emotional activity is much easier to cause than soul activity. But it doesn't prove conversion. I might be able to convince someone to perform a physical or emotional action, but I can't cause someone else's conversion for the simple reason that I cannot cause my own.

If, as the revivalists taught, I could cause my own conversion through a simple act of my will, then I should use every means at my disposal to convince someone else to cause their own conversion. My job would not merely be to faithfully proclaim a message, but to coerce a decision by any means at my disposal. Of course, that's not how the Bible portrays conversion.

To complicate matters further, a missionary has to account for cross-cultural factors that impact evangelism. For example, missionaries who serve among highly impoverished people will have to be aware of the power dynamics that may be at play when they communicate with their national friends. These power dynamics can cause difficulties in evangelism because of the perceived discrepancy of power between themselves and their national friends. Some may seem to respond to Christ when they are simply acquiescing to the suggestions of their powerful, rich missionary friend. This means missionaries need to be even more careful with conversions than other ministers.

"BUT DOESN'T THE BIBLE SAY THAT SOME WILL FALL AWAY?"

I've heard missionaries respond to these kinds of critiques, "If just one new believer comes into the kingdom as a result of revivalism, doesn't that justify these practices?" After all, missionaries observe, the Bible predicts that some will initially believe and then later fall away, suggesting that their spiritual condition never really changed. Meanwhile, the argument goes, others will believe and endure. So it may be sad, but that doesn't mean we should abandon these effective practices altogether.

To be sure, passages like the parable of the soils teach us that some professors will endure in the faith, while others won't. Yet we should hardly construe such passages as giving us *carte blanche* permission to be as careless as we want in declaring assurance of salvation. Carelessly receiving people into a church does impact people's spiritual condition. First, it risks further hardening them against the gospel once they fall away, since they now believe they've "tried Christianity" but found it wanting.

Second, prematurely labelling someone a Christian who isn't can do great communal harm. In many overseas contexts, a person's communal testimony matters more than in the West. Someone who has been baptized as a Christian and yet lives like their old selves will bring great shame to the name of Christ.

Okay, but about the one genuine believer whom God brings into his kingdom through these practices? Doesn't he or she justify the practices that saved them? No. God will use all kinds of things for good, even evil, as he taught through Joseph; or the devil, as he taught through Job (Gen. 50:20). The mere fact that God can and will sometimes use our unwise methods doesn't mean he endorses those methods, any more than he endorses evil or the devil when he employs them.

For these reasons and many others, churches should treat new converts carefully. The Lord Jesus told us to prepare for false conversions. Our missionary strategy should leave room for this possibility. I remember one national woman who was, in good faith, hastily baptized and added to the church. She promptly continued to live her life as if nothing had ever happened to her, even as she remained inside the community of Christians. She was promiscuous with young Christian men and was divisive through gossip and backbiting. After several years, she was eventually removed from the church, but not before multiplying sin in the community and causing much harm to the reputation of Christ.

CONCLUSION

Ultimately, the promises of those old revivalist pastors fell far short of their predictions. The millennium hasn't come yet; awakenings are still extraordinary. After assuring his students that they could render the salvation of their children certain, one revivalist preacher later confessed that he did not know that a single one of his children ever gave "evidence of having been converted" (*Revival and Revivalism*, 289). Just recently, I asked one long-term missionary's opinion of the revivalism being practiced in his area of Asia. "My wife and I are not big fans," he said. "We've seen that the numbers seem to go away pretty quickly."

These sentiments are growing. A leader of a mission agency was invited by his friend to visit a city in East Asia to determine whether he should move there as a missionary. When he visited, he witnessed large gatherings of Christians and those who were interested in the gospel. He couldn't believe it! There was so much Christian activity that he and his wife, who didn't want to build on another's foundation, decided to move elsewhere. Within a few years, his friend called him and begged him to reconsider. The mission leader was shocked as his friend told him the crowds he'd seen with his own eyes were all gone. "What did we see when we were there?" He asked. His friend's response was chilling: "Smoke and mirrors."

I have so many stories like this. When large numbers are reported, there is so much fanfare and celebration. But the correction or retraction of those hasty reports—whether public or in-house—are all too quiet.

So let's ignore revivalism. Let's instead maintain our

devotion to prayer. We should pray that God would move the hearts of our children and the hearts of those we serve. We should pray that he would bring many into his kingdom while we faithfully proclaim Christ. We should pray that he gives an extraordinary measure of his Holy Spirit so that many are added to God's kingdom. There's always the possibility of fruit and blessing while we serve Christ (1 Cor 15:58). And while he gives us the fruit of our labors—much or little—let's make it our aim to find so much joy in him today that the normal activities of prayer, service, and evangelism are a delight!

Revival and Revivalism in Youth Ministry

By Mike McGarry

God's people have always placed a high priority on passing the faith from generation to generation. Both the church and Christian parents have always been called to co-disciple children and teenagers in order to develop life-long faith. So how should we respond when a significant portion of the younger generation is either growing up without any Christian faith or rejecting it after they graduate?

Imagine a church whose preacher delivers faithful expository sermons and whose elders provide trustworthy care over their members. But that church's children walk away from the faith after high school. What good is it to grow a large church only to lose the next generation?

This isn't a new dilemma. In 1917, Frank Otis Erb reflected on the contemporary church's efforts to reach the younger generation: "The democratic spirit led a revolt against absolutism everywhere, religion and intellect not excluded. The final and authoritative doctrines of the church were fiercely assailed by Voltaire and his friends, not least because they were final and authoritative, and those who held them were denounced as ignorant, superstitious, or hypocritical. Freedom of thought was not only demanded but asserted."[111] His analysis of the church's struggle to pass the faith to the next generation sounds alarmingly similar to our own. Erb then proceeded to paint a picture of the church's efforts to seek revival among young people in his day—the remnants of which can still be seen in many youth ministries today.

REVIVALISM IN YOUTH MINISTRY

It's important to recognize and applaud the motivation for these ministries. There was grave concern over worldliness and an increasing apathy toward the things of God. So ministries like the Young People's Society of Christian Endeavor and the Young Men's Christian Association (YMCA) partnered with churches to promote the Christian faith in the next generation. More than 100 years ago, these ministers shared a concern that still rests on today's youth workers: to make adult disciples whose faith took root in their teen years.

---

111 Frank Otis Erb, *The Development of the Young People's Movement* (Chicago, IL: University of CHicago Press, 1917), 1.

A distinct youth culture began to mature in the years that followed World War I. This eventually fed into a generational divide that introduced serious concerns about outside influences on adolescents. Churches and parents were at a loss about how to respond since their tried-and-true methods didn't seem to work anymore. The early days of modern youth ministry were paved by ministries like Young Life and Youth for Christ, who saw themselves as filling a gap the church wouldn't meet. Unchurched teenagers were unlikely to walk into a church, especially when the church mostly ignored them anyway. Instead, they met those teenagers on their own terms. The Young Life model was eventually adopted by church-based youth workers, and Youth for Christ rallies provided the basis for evangelistic events that are still prevalent today.

Much more could be said about youth ministry's development, but here's the point: the shift from smaller, instruction-driven ministry to larger and more evangelistic ministry reflects the difference between revival and revivalism. These differences remain today. I hesitate to paint with a broad brush, but it's generally true: youth ministries that prioritize evangelism and exist outside the local church will trend toward revivalism, while those who emphasize discipleship and seek to support the local church will likely take a more methodical approach.

The influence of Finney's "new measures" can still be seen in youth ministries across the country as they seek revival among GenZ. Retreats and evangelistic rallies often proclaim a gospel that's measured by tearful teenagers raising their hand to pray a prayer more than it's concerned about genuine repentance and confession of sin.

REVIVAL IN YOUTH MINISTRY

Again, the motives of revivalists (for the most part) should be commended: they want young people to come to Jesus. But the theological foundation of revivalism is made of clay and cannot deliver. True and lasting revival isn't built on a platform with lots of fanfare. It never has been. Passing the faith from generation to generation is both simpler and more difficult than revivalists prophesy.

So what do we do? Teach teenagers how to read and understand the Bible. Teach them how to pray. Apply the gospel to their whole lives—their head, heart, and hands. Help them see how the gospel is not just for evangelism, but for the Christian life. Partner with parents to equip them to view their parenting and family-life as discipleship. Integrate students into the life of the church so they know they genuinely belong with their church family. And finally, model repentance when you sin against them.

These aren't sexy or impressive. These strategies won't go viral on social media or get you booked for the main stage at any ministry conferences. In fact, committing yourself to these priorities probably won't make your youth group the largest one in town. But you know what? It will serve your students for the long haul.

The Worship Set: Today's Sawdust Trail

By Drew Hodge

It's hot. The smell of sweat and sawdust is thick in the revival tent. Another stanza of, "Just as I Am" begins and there's no sign of stopping. Some folks are crying, singing, and kneeling. Others are walking down that "Sawdust Trail" of a center aisle to shake the preacher's hand. What was making them move? Was it the sermon, the song, the smell, or the Spirit?

Or was it the music?

The spirit of revivalism is alive and well in many of our church services today. One article in our Journal lists six marks of revivalism. I want to consider how four of those marks are intensified by the way we use music in our gatherings. In particular, I'm concerned we're using the "worship set" to stir up tears and feelings instead of "love and good works" (Heb 10:24).

1: WEAK ECCLESIOLOGY

Without a right understanding of why we gather and what we should do when we gather, we can be taken by the siren song of revivalism. If God really doesn't care what we do when we gather and it's up to us to design a "worship experience," then everything is on the table. We will use whatever means we can to produce our worthwhile ends.

But thankfully, God *does* care what we do when we gather. He hasn't left us to our own devices.

We must be regulated by God's Word and what he has prescribed for the church: singing (Col. 3:16), praying (Acts 2:42), Scripture reading (1 Tim. 4:13), preaching (2 Tim. 4:2), baptizing (Matt. 28:19), and partaking in the Lord's Supper (1 Cor. 11:20).

If we say, "the Bible doesn't prohibit x, y, or z so we can do x, y, or z," then we will be tempted to employ all kinds of methods that aren't useful in the "building up" (1 Cor. 14:26) of the body. If you're a music leader or pastor who holds that position, I have a simple question for you: aren't you exhausted? It's so tiring to constantly reinvent the worship wheel. It's a never-ending cycle.

Instead, we ought to trust in God's good design to build his church through the ordinary means of grace. Thoughtfully ordered worship sets should include more than songs. We should walk through the gospel using prayers, readings, and creeds. Worship is more than music and so a worship set—or a liturgy, or an order of service—must include more than music, too.

2: EMOTION DRIVEN

Music is emotional. God didn't make a mistake in the way he made us to have a visceral response to beauty. And music can be beautiful. Yes, even in corporate worship!

Music is a gift that can be used *or* abused. No matter your musical style or setting—piano and hymns or a band with choruses—we can misuse the gift and beauty of music to accomplish our man-centered goal. Music is used properly when it deploys truth to shepherd our emotions to our heads and hearts. Music is *abused* when it seeks to elicit an emotional response as an end unto itself. If my goal is to get people to *feel something*, then my musical choices will reflect that. I'll stack the "set" with power ballads that pluck all the right heart strings and generate a sense of transcendence in the congregation that can only be described as God coming down.

But did he? Or did I hypnotize you with a minor fall and a major lift? If we get the right sounds in the right order, can we prod the Holy Spirit to move? Can I persuade you to move down the aisle, to pray a prayer? If we don't invite the Holy Spirit into our presence, is he trapped outside?

We can get so caught up in the moment that we start to glory in our singing and not in our Redeemer. If you think you haven't worshiped until you've felt chills or raised your hands, then you'll do almost anything to get that same high again. From the "Sawdust Trail" to Charles Finney's "Mourners Bench" to the more modern, synth-driven "worship set," you can trace a line of emotional pragmatism that has deceived many into thinking they have met with God. But in reality, they likely only met with a kick drum.

Hold up. Am I saying that all emotions are evil and misleading? No, of course not. But they shouldn't be thought of as infallible or unfallen either. And guess what? I'm not even categorically against a synth or a kick drum! If corporate worship is a bus, you don't want emotions in the driver's seat. You want truth driving the bus. Don't leave emotions on the curb. Instead, put them in the passenger's seat, with a seatbelt on.

When emotions are driven by the truth, they can be safe, good, and beautiful. Rightly ordered, our emotions—or, to use a good old Puritan word, our "affections"—are appropriate responses to the truth, goodness, and beauty of God's grace that is greater that all our sin.

3: LIGHTS, CAMERA, ACTION!

As Andrew wrote in his previously mentioned article, "Revivalism is usually marked by a reliance on expertise and professionalism in the execution of the means of revival." In other words, man can produce so-called revival through man-made means and methods.

If we believe it's up to us to *produce* worship, then professionalism, production, and performance will be elevated on our list of priorities. The way we use music and other aesthetics in our gatherings can communicate that the congregation is primarily there to watch.

Am I arguing that high-quality production is all bad? Not necessarily. You don't need lights, smoke, and screens to be "high production." High production can show up in classical settings as well. Poor quality is not a virtue.

Of course, excellence in worship should look different in different churches. Do you lead four-part hymns from a piano? Then do it well to the glory of God. Do you lead half a band of mismatched instruments? Then do it well. Be prepared. Practice to the glory of God. Whatever your musical context, lead in a way that your flock can understand, follow, and participate.

4: A CULT OF PERSONALITY AND PREFERENCE

The title "Worship Leader" grew out of a soil that was tilled by revivalism. If we need one man to usher us into the presence of God to "worship," then that man and his accompanying skills and style are essential to our ability to worship. If you say, "I can't worship unless…" then whatever you say next has become your mediator, a so-called priest that serves as a musical conduit for your engagement with God.

The title also wrongly convolutes music and worship. All of life is worship; all of our gathering is worship—not just the music. Plus, the only man that can usher us into the presence of a holy God is Jesus, and he has already done that through his cross, resurrection, and ascension. He's our mediator and priest—not the music guy.

Does this mean that we should shy away from leaders with personality and talent? Not necessarily. A godly preacher with lots of personality and talent will not completely bury those aspects of himself. Instead, he will submit those things to the word of God and the task of preaching. He will use them as a tool to effectively communicate *God's* truth—not his truth or personality.

A godly and talented music leader does the same thing. How do you know if that's happening? Well, after a sermon or a song, do you think to yourself, "What awesome music!"? Or do you think, "What an awesome God!"?

Here's another litmus-test question: are you easily edified by worship music outside your preferred musical style or tradition? If not, why not? I believe a mature Christian can find the Spirit and truth in diverse worship settings. Let's teach our people how to be mature worshippers.

DOWN THE SAWDUST TRAIL

"Down the Sawdust Trail," written by Millie Lou Pace, is a love song to the event where she believes she was converted. It's an evocative song about the "sinner's cry" and her mother kneeling and praying and hearing "Jesus call." It's a lovely country ballad. It's also bizarre. Why? Because it focuses on the wrong thing. It makes much of her memories and feelings about that one meeting and very little of the gospel.

May the same never be said of us.

Is Being Above Reproach a Qualification?

By Jeffrey Jeffson

Does Paul's requirement that an elder be "above reproach" act as its own qualification, or does Paul mean for it to qualify all the other qualifications—as in, "above reproach by not being adulterous" and "above reproach by not being a drunkard," and so forth?

Since it is first in the list, the most natural reading suggests the answer is both. "Above reproach" is its own qualification, *and* it can be applied to all other qualifications. To be above reproach is different from adultery or drunkenness. It suggests you're *not even open to accusations* of adultery or drunkenness. You're not walking up to the line or making things murky for those watching you.

Our elders were forced to consider this qualification in the heat of the moment. A pastor of our church had not crossed any one line. He had not committed adultery, was not a drunkard, was not a lover of money, was not violent, and so forth. Yet he had conducted himself in a way that was very foolish with respect to one of those other qualifications. You might say his actions showed him to be walking toward one of those lines without crossing it. Several members of the church had raised the matter with elders. He was warned not to repeat such foolish actions. Yet he repeated them, prompting still other people to raise them with elders.

And all this, we decided, indicated he was *below* reproach, even though he formally met all the other qualifications. His folly had made him easily *accusable*, such that accusations had a ring of truth. He had lost credibility as a minister of God's Word. Therefore, we asked him to resign.

HOW OTHERS DEFINE THE PHRASE

The process of getting to that decision was not easy. We eventually reached unanimity in asking him to resign, but that took a while, and we had to search out what different commentators had said. We found the following discussions especially helpful:

- "Since all God's people are called to live holy and blameless lives (Phil. 2:15, 1 Thess. 5:23), since the world casts a critical eye at the Christian community (1 Pet. 3:15-16), and since Christian leaders lead primarily by their example (1 Pet. 5:3), an irreproachable life is indispensable to the Christian leader."
- "Slightly different but related to 'respectable' (*koismos* in 1 Tim. 3:2) which 'conveys ideas of self-control, proper behavior, orderliness.'"
- "As low-bar as 'above reproach' may sound in some ears, with just a little reflection we can discover some of the wisdom in it. This banner qualification is not merely 'innocent' or 'righteous' or 'acquitted', but 'above reproach.' We are looking for men *above* being reasonably charged with wrong in the first place."
- "The term means, writes commentator George Knight, 'not open to attack or criticism' (*The Pastoral Epistles*, 155); 'he is not objectively chargeable' (156). He's not one who makes a practice of dancing around the fine line of righteous reproach."

- "Since Paul is writing to pastors of local churches, it stands to reason that the arbiters of whether an overseer is 'above reproach' are those on the local level who are close enough to attest (or contest) a man's character. The gist: your elders and pastors should be examples of godly graces and Christian maturity."
- "Take heed to yourselves, lest your example contradict your doctrine, and lest you lay such stumbling blocks before the blind, as may be the occasion of their ruin; lest you unsay with your lives, what you say with your tongues; and be the greatest hinderers of the success of your own labors … one proud, surly, lordly word, one needless contention, one covetous action, may cut the throat of many a sermon, and blast the fruit of all that you have been doing."
- "'*Anepilemptos*' (above reproach) means 'not able to be held…' In Titus 1:6 the same idea of being above reproach is conveyed, but a different term (*anengletos* — 'unreprovable') is used."
- "The all-too-common practice today is to forgive a leader who sins and immediately restore him to his ministry. The church, like God, must not hesitate to forgive those who truly repent. To immediately restore them to the ministry, however, lowers the standard that God expects leaders to follow."

HOW WE SUMMARIZED THE QUALIFICATION

After all this study, we summarized the qualification "above reproach" for ourselves with these points:

- There should be no reason for the elders or congregation to question the character or integrity of a pastor.
- Discerning the credibility of any accusation should never be a matter of personal favor or affection for the pastor. Reproach should be discerned objectively for the sake of stewarding the office.
- A pastor should not have to be repeatedly reproved on

matters of his personal conduct or in regards to maintaining accountability.
- The primary responsibility for being above reproach is laid on the pastor himself. Elders of the church (and members) do not bear the primary burden of defending his choices.
- Falling below reproach as a qualification does not usually happen in a moment. It is discerned over time. Not all sin is disqualifying. Some sin can be repented of and allow a pastor to continue in ministry.

It took our elders much discussion and prayer to come to a unified place of understanding. But a clarifying moment came when we stopped to ask ourselves, "Why are we even needing to have this conversation?" It wasn't simply because someone had made an accusation; it was because the brother's own choices and the nature of his actions were clearly foolish (we all agreed on that), such that the accusations were credible. The very fact that we were laboring so long about the matter was evidence to us that he was *below* reproach. He did not have our collective confidence any longer.

Our elders had to consider how to obey Christ's call for overseers to be above reproach in real time. If possible, you want to have this conversation with your elders before it happens.

HOW TO COMMUNICATE TO THE CONGREGATION

When it came time to communicate the matter to the congregation, we wondered how much to share. We needed to communicate that he had fallen *below* reproach, yet not unnecessarily drag our brother into further public disrepute.

It was a challenge for the elders to discern the level of "trust us" when it came to sharing the details of the accusations, since there was no overtly disqualifying behavior (adultery, drunkenness, etc.). We had nothing to hide. But the matter did not necessarily require all details to come forward. It was a challenge for some members to grasp "falling below reproach" being a reason to accept a resignation from a pastor they love. We made ourselves very accessible for conversations and clarification as possible.

The entire event was disorienting at times because the matter of reproach is not as easily discernible as graver sins. This all required unity, wisdom, and labor in prayer by the pastors. It required patience, trust, and fiercely upholding the Word of God by the congregation.

This is the qualification of the pastor: no accusation thrown at him should have any stickiness to it after appropriate investigation. Sadly, sometimes the most trusted pastors commit the gravest sins. It surprises us, shocks us, and hurts us. Sometimes accusations against a pastor turn out to be untrue. But sometimes a pastor dances around the fine line of righteous reproach to the point he cannot be trusted with the ministry of the Word and oversight of the church. That's what it means to say he's not "above reproach."

What Does Being 'Above Reproach' Mean?

By Paul Alexander

If the elder qualification lists in 1 Timothy 3 and Titus 1 were undoubtedly exhaustive, we could simply say that being above reproach means meeting every qualification in both lists.

Yet since the lists are different (and don't even include all the fruit of the Spirit in Galatians 5), we are wiser to conclude that the lists are intended to be representative, rather than exhaustive, and so we probably should not use the lists as definitive. Being above reproach, then, is probably more than just checking off the items on these virtue lists. But it's not less.

To be above reproach is, arguably, the most general of all the elder qualifications, so it has to be defined more generally. A good start might be to say that it means being beyond reach of any criticism or accusation that, if true, would either disqualify a man from office for aberrant conviction, deficient character, or sinful outward conduct; or would cast serious doubt on the credibility of his own personal profession of faith in Jesus and the reality of his repentance. He certainly is not sinless, but neither does his example invite the kind of disparagement that undermines his public ministry or the testimony of the church he serves.

Of course, the condition "if true" is important. After all, both staff and non-staff elders are targets for all kinds of unjust criticisms. The public character and moral authority of the office inevitably invites discontent from all directions. If defined too carelessly or broadly, the very generality of the qualification could be weaponized as a catch-all reason for dismissing elders for differences in personality, opinion, morality, and doctrine.

Lest we forget, Jesus himself bore reproach. There is, then, something of a necessity to bearing the right kind of reproach in the Christian life and ministry, while bearing that unjust reproach with an attitude, demeanor, and comportment that is itself above reproach.

The bare reality of reproach toward an elder does not necessarily mean he is no longer above it. Members of churches, even majorities, can wrongly criticize and disparage an elder. This is why the reason for reproach must be serious, clear, outward, verified, and biblically delineated.

We might also say that above reproach means not being guilty of any clear character flaw or verified outward behavior that would bring the truth of the gospel or the holiness of the church into disrepute if publicly known. An elder's character and conduct cannot clearly or consistently contradict his profession of faith, or his proclamation of the faith. No clear character defect comes immediately to mind when you think of him.

Perhaps we may not like his personality or resonate with how he communicates. We may resent his rebukes or chafe at his correction. But then we'd be wrong, not him.

How 'Above Reproach' Lay Elders Saved My Ministry

By Gary Kirst

A special elders' meeting was called. This time, I, as the senior pastor, was the subject of concern.

Our lay elders had detected flashes of unhealthy, fleshly pride in me. They wanted to nip these things in the bud—things like secretly and unilaterally making ministry decisions I knew our other two staff pastors would object to or avoiding certain difficult pastoral calls because I knew they would cause offense (yes, I wanted to be liked).

There was actually quite a laundry list of offenses. After nine years of ministry in that church, this was the first time I experienced anything close to such a grilling.

As my offenses were enumerated, I felt my blood pressure skyrocket. I had a comeback for each perceived offense. My reflex was absolute defensiveness.

But then I looked into the faces of these four or five men. I knew them. I knew their track records of humble, faithful, loving service in our church. They were the kind of men who, if they slipped in displaying the fruits of the Spirit, they wouldn't slip for long and would humbly repent. They cared so deeply about their own walks with the Lord and the health of our church. And any serious accusation, if leveled against them, simply couldn't stick.

These men, though imperfect, were above reproach. I knew that. And now they were unified in confronting me for my foolish pride. By God's grace, at that crucial moment, I reasoned, "If these men say I have a problem with pride, then I better get to repenting."

Now, had these men not been qualified elders, it would have been so much easier to go tit for tat with them. And chances are I would have left and sought out a different church "more appreciative of my gifts."

But there was power in their holy lives. The Lord of the church was speaking through them to get through to a young pastor who thought too highly of himself. I'm forever grateful for that biblical prescription, "An overseer must be above reproach," as I pastor that same church 21 years later. Without those men, I'm not sure my ministry would have survived.

Why is Being Above Reproach Necessary in Hard Times?

By David Doran

Claire sits before the jury with a dry mouth, her heart beating at a jogging pace. The courtroom buzzes with intensity about a situation she knows nothing of and has no desire to learn about. She's in the room for one reason: to tell the jury whether her experience of her friend matches the narrative being presented. The facts of the case are not hers to weigh. Claire is there to weigh a reputation against a story—she's a character witness.

The congregation of God's Spirit-filled people are called into a similar moment as they examine a potential pastor. The timeline is out of order—no crime has been committed nor accusations leveled. Still, they are called to testify to the character of a man.

This is the God-breathed wisdom of Paul instructing Timothy to establish the leadership of the church. Paul calls for pastors to be "above reproach." This phrase forms a heading for the rest of the qualifications. Paul calls men into authority who have a loving track record of authority in every arena. Paul calls the church to embrace submission to men who demonstrate self-control and sacrifice for the good of others as their modus operandi.

Why?

Because the enemy is an accuser. The battlefield of ministry is messy. There will be days of hard decisions and heartache. When the dust settles on those challenging moments, many won't have all the facts. Many will want to understand but won't—and can't.

In those moments, there will be a deep need for trust. Sheep must trust the Chief Shepherd most. And they will also need to trust the under-shepherds they have called.

The congregation will need to remember their own character witness. Are they omniscient? Of course not. But they can prayerfully be comforted by the character of the pastors they've appointed, and the pastors' track record of faithfulness and Spirit-filled living. As the old saying goes, "Past action is the best indicator of future action."

There will be days when the going gets tough. At that time, you won't need a tough leader, but one who is tough to accuse.

By God's grace, you want shepherds who live with such obvious Spirit-dependence and fruit that false accusations fall flat. The church searches for men whose past faithfulness layers future confusions with trust.

In our day and age, we've traded character for charisma and faithfulness for fast-growing. Many churches surge on the back of charisma. Sadly, many of the same have stumbled under the burden of unhealthy leadership. Perhaps we will learn and return to the biblical model.

Why Does a Pastor Being 'Above Reproach' Matter?

By Peter Hess

Several years back, a journalist named David Castro had this to say about whether moral failings should disqualify individuals from public service:

> Moral failings by themselves do not render politicians unserviceable. It is possible for political leaders to be extremely effective and do good work, despite moral and ethical shortcomings. Such frailties do not necessarily impede the practice of politics. It is the public reaction to such failings that causes the problem in effectiveness. ... It is more important for the people themselves to own their system and ask the flawed individuals within it to make progress than to continue a childish search for perfect role models who do not exist and never have.[112]

---

[112] From an article by David Castro entitled "As Weiner Falls: Reflecting on Character, Morals, and Political Leadership. Accessed online at http://www.dailykos.com/story/2013/08/13/1230580/-As-Weiner-Falls-Reflecting-on-Character-Morals-and-Political-Leadership# on 05/10/2022.

Amazingly, Castro cast the blame for the ineffectiveness of "morally-challenged" political leaders not on the damage caused by the leaders themselves, but on what Castro considered the "childish" response of the general public to those moral failures.

While I wholeheartedly disagree with Castro's perspective, I think we need to admit that his view represents the new public consensus. In the eyes of many, it is no longer character that counts, but whether or not the leader can "get the job done."

That perspective on leadership may prevail in the world, but it must never prevail in the church. In the church of Jesus Christ, character matters for leadership. No character, no qualification to lead.

The clearest place to see this is 1 Timothy 3:2, where Paul writes this about the character required for overseers (elders/pastors): "Therefore an overseer must be above reproach."

Being "above reproach" is the first in a list of qualifications for the man who aspires to serve as an elder in the local church. Really, being "above approach" is a summary qualification. All the other qualifications of 1 Tim. 3:2-7—one-woman man, self-controlled, sensible, respectable, hospitable, apt to teach, sober, gentle, peace-loving, and generous—really serve to flesh out what being "above reproach" looks like.

We can summarize the list this way. An elder is a man against whom no one can lodge a serious criticism. The idea is that there is no aspect of his life that people could look at and reproach him for being a _____ man (you fill in the blank: dishonest, greedy, lustful, worldly, etc). And Paul is strong here. He says that an elder *must* (in the Greek, *dei*, "it is necessary") be "above reproach." In other words, it is better to have no elders than to appoint men who are not "above reproach."

Why is this the case? Why is the first qualification for pastors that they be "above reproach"? It's simple. Unlike modern politicians, pastors aren't in the efficiency business. Pastors are called by God to help others become like Jesus. And you can't give away what you don't possess.

So along with David Castro, the world may bask in its immoral but efficient leaders. But it must never be that way in the church. Those who lead the church must be "above reproach"—not perfect, but not detrimentally flawed—not sinless, but obviously sanctified.

BOOK REVIEW:

The Heart of the Gospel:

A.B. SIMPSON, THE FOURFOLD GOSPEL, AND LATE NINETEENTH-CENTURY EVANGELICAL THEOLOGY, BY BERNIE A. VAN DE WALLE

By Kevin Niebuhr

Maya Angelou once said, "*You can't really know where you are going until you know where you have been.*" She's right. If we desire to understand the present, we profit from learning about the past.

And yet the difficult part about gazing into our past is that there are periods we'd rather forget. I'm still grateful that no one had camera phones to document my early 90s grunge phase. For many pastors and Christians, the latter half of the nineteenth century tends to be one of phases we'd rather forget.

Most of my brothers in ministry love reflecting on the First Great Awakening. Our shelves are full of books by and about men like Jonathan Edwards and George Whitefield. This time in the history of the American church is encouraging and inspiring to many, especially in a day and age when the American church desperately needs revival. And yet I doubt many pastors have a host of books on what transpired just a century later. The Second Great Awakening—a misnomer to many—saw the rise of religious fervor sweep across the country due in large part to manufactured, premeditated "revivals" led by men like Charles Finney.

Many pastors possess at best a superficial knowledge of this era; sadly, some are wholly ignorant of it. While many books on this period either champion the revivalists' methodology or denounce their efforts, Bernie Van De Walle takes an entirely different approach. His scholarly work *The Heart of the Gospel* focuses not on nineteenth century revivalism but rather on the theology of the men behind the movement, most notably A.B. Simpson.

A.B. SIMPSON

A.B. Simpson (1843–1919), the reluctant founder of the Christian & Missionary Alliance, was a Canadian Presbyterian minister who eventually left his denomination after coming under the influence of the holiness movement. Simpson's heart for missions and reaching the unreached led him to move to New York, where he began a preaching ministry focusing on immigrant dock workers. To this end, he started various ecumenical parachurch ministries. Van De Wall states that Simpson's desire wasn't to create "an ecclesiastical body, but a fraternal body of believers, in cordial harmony with Christians of every name."[113]

Simpson recognized that literature, if well produced, could help him achieve this goal. His *Fourfold Gospel* and the theology behind it were widely distributed and became influential in shaping the ministry that dominated nineteenth-century American evangelicalism. It also birthed the Pentecostal movement. While Simpson would be better described as a charismatic evangelist with a heart for missions, not a revivalist, it's not hard to see how he was a crucial figure in fueling the revivalism of his day.

---

113 Christian Alliance, Christian Alliance Yearbook (1888), 48

THE HEART OF THE GOSPEL: THE FOURFOLD GOSPEL

J.I. Packer once said, "I am one of those who believe that this notion [penal substitution] takes us to the very heart of the Christian gospel."[114] The *heart* of the gospel, to be clear, is the message of Christ bearing the wrath of God meant for sinful mankind so that man could be declared righteous.

Yet Van De Walle uses that phrase to summarize all four parts of Simpson's "fourfold gospel": Christ is our Savior (soteriology), our Sanctifier (sanctification), our Healer (continuationism), and our Coming King (eschatology). It's an enlarged heart, one might say, which inevitably shifts what people will count as most important, as we'll see in a moment.

Van De Walle observes that this gospel was proclaimed throughout this period of time by men like D.L. Moody in Chicago, A.J. Gordon in Boston, and A.T. Pierson in Philadelphia, which then shaped their methodology and ministry tactics.

CHRIST OUR SAVIOR

To begin with, Simpson's understanding of "Christ Our Savior" impacted how a revivalist like him would plan, coordinate, and execute revivals. Van de Walle states: "At the heart of late nineteenth-century revivalistic soteriology was a belief in the freedom and ability of the human will" (p. 26). Simpson and other nineteenth-century revivalists pursued revivals on the firm basis that, while mankind has total depravity, he does not have total inability. Man's ability to freely choose God drove them to believe revival could be systematically implemented under the right conditions.

This assumption was different than that of an earlier generation of revivalists like Jonathan Edwards, observes Van De Walle: "[Jonathan Edwards] believed the revivals of the eighteenth-century to be unexpected, altogether independent, and even surprising' works of God." He also adds that Edwards firmly believed "no human action can stimulate revival.

---

[114] J.I. Packer, "What Did the Cross Achieve?" (1973) Tyndale Biblical Theology Lecture

It remains the exclusive work of God" (p. 25). Edwards' view contrasts sharply with Simpson's contemporaries who "believed that while revival may be sparked by or flow from some miraculous event, revival itself is the result of both human decision and divine action. Revival involves nothing more miraculous than humanity's engaging in the right use of the [divinely] constituted means. … If the means were rightly implemented, revival would follow" (p. 26).

CHRIST OUR SANCTIFIER, HEALER, AND COMING KING

Van De Walle doesn't spend too much time explaining how Simpson's other three positions also drive revivalistic methodology. Nonetheless, they are useful if you want a comprehensive picture of what was happening during this period of church history. For example, Van De Walle explains that Simpson's doctrine of sanctification (which was heavily influenced by the Holiness Movement) points to a common theme in nineteenth-century revivalism: the shift of focus from justification (as espoused by Whitefield and Edwards) to sanctification. The holiness movement and its belief in total sanctification and higher life theology had shifted the voice of the revivalist. "*You can be justified through Christ!*" had turned into a different promise: "*You can be totally sanctified through Christ!*"

Van De Walle also looks at the positions of "Christ Our Healer" and "Christ our Coming King". Simpson's continuationism and promises of divine healing drove flocks of hurting people to these meetings in hopes of experiencing physical healing. His hope of a coming king helped raise up a new generation of Christians who held to premillennial eschatology.

I try to be charitable in the books that I read. I don't want to only read books from "my camp." At the same time, I don't appreciate ad hominem attacks, fallacious strawman arguments, and mischaracterization of my theological positions. Who does! Gratefully, Van De Walle, though he agrees with the revivalist's methods, does good history as he faithfully presents the men from both their First and Second Awakenings, their convictions, their influences, and their methods in an unbiased way.

Spurgeon once said, "I am not an admirer of the peculiar views of Mr. Finney, but I have no doubt that he was useful to many."[115] While I'm not an admirer of all the positions and practices Simpson had throughout his lifetime, I am grateful for Van De Walle's scholarly work. He presents greater insight into this man and presents his research in such a way that the reader can walk away with a better understanding of where we have been so that we can better see where we are going.

---

115 Charles Spurgeon, "Lectures to my Students" page 185

BOOK REVIEW:

Revival and Revivalism:

THE MAKING AND MARRING OF AMERICAN EVANGELICALISM, 1750-1858, BY IAIN MURRAY

By Bobby Jamieson

"How did we get here?" is a question that is always relevant and often illuminating. Yet contemporary evangelicals don't ask it as often as we should.

In his book *Revival and Revivalism: The Making and Marring of American Evangelicalism, 1750-1858*, Iain Murray tells a story that helps explain how evangelicals—Baptists, Presbyterians, Methodists, and more—got to where we are today.

FROM REVIVAL . . .

The book's title tells the whole story in a nutshell. Over the one hundred and nine years Murray examines, from 1750 to 1858, American evangelicals' understanding and experience of evangelism morphed from "revival" to "revivalism."

Background: The First Great Awakening

Not that what came before 1750 wasn't important. From about 1735 to 1740, under the preaching of Jonathan Edwards, George Whitefield, and others, the American colonies experienced a massive spiritual enlivening which came to be known as the First Great Awakening. This phenomenon was driven by preaching that emphasized the biblical truths of the holiness of God, the gravity of sin, man's enslavement to sin, and the need for the Holy Spirit to give new birth so that people might repent, believe, and be saved.

Though superficial responses to such preaching inevitably got mixed up with the true, contemporaries of these events regarded them as a genuine revival. They believed this spiritual movement had been caused by God's sovereign choice to pour out his Spirit in a profound and unusual way, thus causing the ordinary, biblically appointed means of evangelism to bear extraordinary fruit.

Heirs of Edwards and Whitefield

Murray's story, then, begins with the heirs of the First Great Awakening who ministered from New England to Virginia, men such as Samuel Davies and Alexander McWhorter (chs. 1-4). These pastors held to the same theology that drove Edwards' and Whitefield's preaching, and they had been personally impacted by the events of 1735-1740. Throughout the second half of the eighteenth century, these men and the ministers who followed them periodically experienced the blessing of God on their ministries in ways that also merited the label "revival."

Revival: Gift of God, not Guaranteed Result

Like their predecessors, these pastors knew that revivals were the sovereign work of God and could not be explained in any other way. Therefore, they preached the gospel, pleaded with sinners, and prayed for fruit like they had for years; and for reasons known only to God, he sometimes blessed these labors remarkably, and sometimes he didn't.

These revivals, in other words, were neither planned by men nor achieved by men. They did not involve any unusual or novel evangelistic techniques. They were understood, therefore, to be gifts of God.

. . . TO REVIVALISM

Then, beginning around 1800, revival began to break out on a greater scale across the young nation, from the northeast to the western states of Kentucky and Tennessee. And what's truly remarkable is that this large-scale revival continued in one form or another for about thirty years, rightly earning it the title of the Second Great Awakening.

The Second Great Awakening

In the beginning, this revival was understood in the same terms as previous ones. Yet over time, theological and practical shifts began to occur that amounted to a revolution by the revival's end. (For this part of the story, see chapters 5 through 12.)

For example, in 1800 in Cane Ridge, Kentucky the Presbyterians' outdoor "communion seasons" (which followed a traditional Scottish practice) became the flashpoint for what looked like a major movement of the Spirit. The meetings grew quickly. Ministers from other denominations, such as the Methodists, shared in the preaching. Large numbers of people who were unaffiliated with any church traveled great distances to come and hear. Many people responded to the preaching and singing, sometimes in disruptively dramatic ways.

Eventually, the leaders of these meetings divided over how to respond to excessive displays of emotion in these meetings. Some—most of the Presbyterians—thought such displays should be permitted or rebuked depending on the case, while others—the Methodists—tended to treat all of them as proof of the work of God's Spirit.

From this point, the Methodist leaders of this work in Kentucky took a strategy that was originally a *response* to revival—namely, protracted outdoor meetings—and made it a key component of their efforts to bring about revival. Further, these Methodists and some others, undergirded by a radically different doctrine of conversion, began to focus their efforts on inducing outward, immediate responses to the gospel.

Two Major Shifts

The story runs along similar lines elsewhere. By the 1820s and 1830s, two major shifts had occurred throughout American evangelicalism.

The first is a doctrinal shift regarding conversion. Up to 1800, evangelicals almost universally believed and preached that God must sovereignly give someone a new nature to enable him or her to repent and believe. By the 1830s, this was widely replaced by an understanding of conversion in which the decision to repent and believe lay entirely within an individual's own power.

This led to (or, in some cases, followed) a shift in evangelistic practice. Many evangelicals adopted practices that sought to bring about an immediate decision. The "anxious bench," the altar call, singling people out personally in public prayer, warning hearers to respond immediately or else lose their chance to repent—all these practices and more grew out of the new belief that conversion is something within a person's power to achieve, or even to effect in others.

The Result: Revivalism

The result of these two shifts is that church leaders began to regard revival as something that could be infallibly secured through the use of proper means—"proper" being whatever would induce an immediate decision or external token of decision. This understanding was most vigorously promoted by Charles Finney, but by the end of the Second Great Awakening it had become a given among a strong majority of American evangelicals. Historian William McLoughlin even went so far as to say that by the mid-nineteenth century, this new system was the national religion of the United States (277).

Thus, revivalism was born. To be sure, revivalism grew up in the soil of genuine revival. But this new practice of revivalism radically differed from the previous understanding of revival it so quickly supplanted. A "revival" became synonymous with a meeting designed to promote revival. Unlike previous generations, evangelicals after 1830 gained the ability, so to speak, to put a revival on the calendar months in advance.

The goal of such revivals was to secure as many immediate decisions for Christ as possible. As such, awareness of the possibility of false conversion seemed to simply vanish from the evangelical consciousness. Few asked whether their new measures just might create as many false converts as true disciples.

SEVEN LESSONS FOR PASTORS

At the risk of stating the obvious, it doesn't take too much effort to see how we got from the 1830s to the evangelistic practices that many of us take for granted today.[1] That holds true whether we're thinking of stadium-based crusades or churches which seek to recreate that atmosphere every Sunday.

Yet, as Murray rightly argues in the book's final chapter, this type of revivalism and the theology that supports it represent a serious departure from both a biblical doctrine of conversion and a biblical practice of evangelism. Therefore, *Revival and Revivalism* should inspire us to reflect critically and carefully about our churches and our evangelistic practices.

Toward that end, here are seven lessons from the book that should be especially relevant for pastors.

1. Don't Confuse an External Act with Inward Change.

First, don't confuse an external act with inward change. Murray writes about the beginnings of the altar call,

Nobody, at first, claimed to regard it as a means of conversion. But very soon, and inevitably, answering the call to the altar came to be confused with being converted. People heard preachers plead for them to come forward with the same urgency with which they pleaded for them to repent and believe. (186; see also 366)

It's possible to walk an aisle, pray a "sinner's prayer," and do any number of other activities without being converted. And it's possible to be converted without taking any of those particular outward steps (though of course conversion will always manifest itself in visible fruit).

Therefore, pastors should not speak about any external action as if it were identical with conversion. And they should be wary of evangelism techniques which seem to equate the two.

2. Beware of Producing False Converts.

Second, beware of producing false converts. Of course it's inevitable that some people who initially profess faith will later prove unrepentant, but pastors can evangelize in a way that either minimizes or multiplies false converts. For instance, Murray cites Samuel Miller to the effect that the anxious seat (precursor to the altar call) promotes "the rapid multiplication of superficial, ignorant, untrained professors of religion"—that is, false converts (366).

3. Be Cautious about Giving Immediate Assurance of Salvation.

Third, be cautious about giving immediate assurance of salvation. Perseverance, as the New Hampshire Confession says, is the grand mark of a true Christian (Heb. 3:6, 14). Faith makes itself known by its fruits—whether good or bad, true or false (Matt. 7:15-27). Yet Murray points out that the new revivalistic methods were actually founded on the promise of immediate assurance:

But the anxious-seat evangelism wanted to do away with any doubts in those who made the public response. The whole strength of its appeal…lay in its suggestion that a response would ensure salvation. To have conceded that there was no sure connection between answering a public appeal and being converted would have been to undermine the whole system. (368)

In other words, the whole point of the new methods was that a response guaranteed salvation. And on that basis, preachers assured people of their salvation immediately and unreservedly simply for coming forward at the end of the service.

Assurance of salvation is possible for the youngest and weakest Christian, but it should always be grounded in the objective work of Christ and corroborated by the fruit of a transformed life.

So pastors, be cautious about giving immediate assurance of salvation. And be careful not to give it on the wrong basis.

4. Tether your Ministry to What God Requires in his Word.

Fourth, tether your ministry to what God requires in his Word. In some ways, the crucial turning point in Murray's narrative comes when the early nineteenth-century Methodists came to regard certain novel, extra-biblical practices—long-duration outdoor camp meetings, techniques to secure immediate decisions, and so on—as the crucial keys to producing conversions (184).

Certainly, Christians are free to pursue evangelism in ways that are not directly exampled in Scripture. If Paul could rent the hall of Tyrannus (Acts 19:9), why shouldn't modern evangelicals evangelize in stadiums?

But the catch is that these new methods became mandates. They became magic bullets. And they became the givens without which people could not imagine anyone getting saved.

Instead, place your confidence in what God has required you to do—preach the Word. Trust that God has given you, in his Word, what you need to be a faithful pastor. Labor with the tools he's given, and trust that he will cause your work to bear fruit.

5. Make Sure your Theology Drives your Practice, not Vice Versa.

Fifth, make sure your theology drives your practice, not vice versa. Murray writes about the spread of the altar call among Baptists, who in the early 19th century were almost unanimously reformed in their soteriology:

> It had not captured anything like the majority of the churches in the 1830s but there can be no doubt that, with the Baptists also, it was the alleged success of the new evangelism which hastened both its adoption and the gradual doctrinal shift to justify it. (325-326)

In this case the practical tail wagged the theological dog. The logic of the new evangelism worked its way into their theological system and rewrote the DNA. Without realizing it, huge numbers of Baptists adopted an evangelistic method that was not only at odds with their theological commitments, but eventually undid them.

6. Don't Equate Outward Success with a Divine Endorsement.

Sixth, don't equate outward success with a divine endorsement. During the conflicts Murray chronicles between the old guard and the new, the revivalists often played the trump card of outward success (282). As one contemporary pastor has famously put it, "Never criticize what God is blessing."

The first problem with the argument from success is that "success" is not always success. Murray writes, "What was indisputable was that making 'conversion' a matter of instant, public decision, with ascertainable numbers immediately announced in the religious press, produced a display of repeated 'successes' on a scale never before witnessed" (283).

But how many of these "decisions" represented genuine conversions? How many were baptized, joined churches, and began new lives? If the numbers back then match the numbers generated through similar methods today, the likely answer is, "Not many."

The second problem with the argument from success is that, in one way or another, God is always blessing us in spite of ourselves. Every time God uses a pastor's preaching to convert people, he's blessing that man's work in spite of that man's sins and errors. So how can you be sure that God is blessing a ministry *because* of some new method rather than *in spite of it*?

Certainly we should expect God to bless preaching and practices that are in line with his Word. But we can't reduce his workings to the mechanics of "most faithful" = "most blessing." Nor can we work backwards from apparent success to discern what must be correct theology and practice.

7. Celebrate the Normal.

Murray writes of the earlier generation of ministers who regarded revival as a gift from God, "The men of the Old School, while believing in revival as fervently as they did…nevertheless knew no biblical reason to be cast down by the normal" (385). These men knew that most of the time, ministry is slow and plodding work. They knew that some sow and others reap. They "believed that God would grant his blessing in the measure that was appropriate—whether in its heightened form…or in quieter ways" (385).

So, finally, don't be discouraged by slow-ripening fruit. Instead, rely on God to work through the regular means of grace. Celebrate the normal.

GOOD REASONS WHY IT'S ALREADY BECOMING A CLASSIC

As I hope this review has proved, there are many good reasons why *Revival and Revivalism* is already becoming a classic. It's long, dense, and somewhat rambling, but it more than repays the time and effort it takes to get through it. I commend it to all present and aspiring church leaders, and to any Christian who likes to ask, "How did we get here?"

[1] For an insightful piece that covers much of the same ground Murray does and also traces this trajectory into the present, see Owen Strachan's article in this issue of the 9Marks Journal.

Made in the USA
Middletown, DE
24 May 2022